9/17

Libya

Libya

BY TERRI WILLIS

Enchantment of the World™
Second Series

CHILDREN'S PRESS®

An Imprint of Scholastic Inc.

Frontispiece: **Sahara Desert**

Consultant: Jacob Mundy, PhD, Assistant Professor of Peace and Conflict Studies, Colgate University, Hamilton, New York
Please note: All statistics are as up-to-date as possible at the time of publication.

Book production by The Design Lab

Library of Congress Cataloging-in-Publication Data
Names: Willis, Terri, author.
Title: Libya / by Terri Willis.
Description: New York : Children's Press, an imprint of Scholastic Inc.,
    2017. | Series: Enchantment of the world | Updated edition. | Includes
    bibliographical references and index.
Identifiers: LCCN 2016047899 | ISBN 9780531235744 (library binding)
Subjects: LCSH: Libya—Juvenile literature.
Classification: LCC DT215 .W55 2017 | DDC 961.2—dc23

1 2 3 4 5 6 7 8 9 10 R 27 26 25 24 23 22 21 20 19 18

Tuareg man in Ghadames

Contents

Left to right: **Father and daughter, Tuareg girl, camels, Mediterranean coast, Nafusa Mountains**

CHAPTER 1

Striving for Freedom

L IFE IN LIBYA HAS OFTEN BEEN CHALLENGING. Its location is outstanding. The nation lies in northern Africa, providing access to both ports on the Mediterranean Sea and trade routes across the Sahara Desert. Because of this, outsiders have often fought the Libyan people for their land. For centuries, Libyans lived under the rule of one foreign invader after another.

In the mid-1900s Libya became an independent nation. Still, its citizens couldn't choose their own leaders. First they had a king. Then the king was ousted by a dictator. That dictator, Muammar Qaddafi, ruled the nation with an iron fist for forty-two years. But in 2011, in the midst of a bloody revolution, he was thrown out of power and murdered.

Opposite: **A truck drives through a rocky stretch of desert in southwestern Libya.**

Battles between groups fighting for control of Libya have left parts of cities such as Benghazi (above) in ruins.

Even though Qaddafi is gone, Libyans still face hard times. Without Qaddafi, no one is in charge. Many groups are fighting for control, and Libyan citizens are caught in the middle. Regular bombings, air strikes, and sniper attacks disrupt their lives. Thousands have been killed.

The United Nations, an international organization dedicated to promoting peace and security, estimates that nearly one-third of Libya's population has been directly affected by the violence. In addition, there is often little food, basic utilities such as electricity and water systems don't always work, and transportation is unreliable. Many hospitals are under-staffed, jobs are scarce, and banks have no cash.

There is hope for Libya, though. People can still imagine an end to the violence, and they are working to achieve peace and justice, even if it comes slowly. Much of the peace movement within Libya is led by young people. Hajer Sharief was

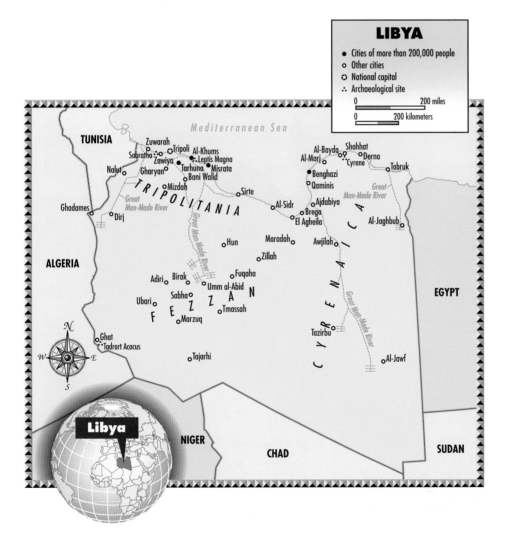

LIBYA

- Cities of more than 200,000 people
- Other cities
- National capital
- Archaeological site

0   200 miles
0   200 kilometers

Mediterranean Sea

TUNISIA

Zuwarah
Tripoli
Al-Khums
Sabratha Zawiya Leptis Magna
Nalut Gharyan Tarhuna Misrata
Bani Walid
Mizdah

TRIPOLITANIA

Ghadames
Great Man-Made River
Dirj

Sirte
Al-Sidr

Al-Bayda Shahhat
Al-Marj   Derna
Cyrene
Tobruk
Benghazi
Qaminis
Great Man-Made River
Ajdabiya
Brega
El Agheila
Al-Jaghbub

ALGERIA

Hun
Maradah
Zillah
Awjilah

Great Man-Made River

Adiri Birak
Umm al-Abid
Fuqaha

Ubari Sabha
FEZZAN Tmassah
Marzuq

EGYPT

CYRENAICA

Tazirbu

Ghat
Tadrart Acacus

Tajarhi

Al-Jawf

Libya

N
W   E
S

NIGER

CHAD

SUDAN

awarded the Student Peace Award of 2017 by the Norwegian Students' and Academics' International Assistance Fund. Born in 1993, Sharief began working for children's and women's rights during the 2011 revolution. When a teenage friend was killed while fighting for democracy, she was motivated to work even harder. Sharief cofounded Together We Build It, an organization that makes sure women are included in Libya's government and peace process.

Another Libyan, Asma Khalifa, was twenty-seven when she won the 2016 Luxembourg Peace Prize as the Outstanding

Girls take part in a demonstration against Muammar Qaddafi in 2011. A wide array of Libyans joined the protests against Qaddafi's dictatorial rule.

Youth Peace Maker. Khalifa grew up in Libya with an abusive father, under an abusive dictator, but knew in her heart that violence wasn't right. Though she opposed Qaddafi, she didn't want to carry a weapon during the revolution. Instead, she volunteered in a hospital, helping the rebels. When she saw that they, too, were committing crimes, she was troubled. Both sides, she felt, were wrong. So she began working with communities, promoting women's rights and peace.

Her nonviolent protest methods are not always accepted. "Many are unconvinced that nonviolence is the way to go. I understand them because I am asking activists not to use guns to protect themselves against armed militias," she said.

Khalifa continues to devote herself to doing training and research on peace making and nonviolent resistance. "If I want to see hope in Libya again, I have to work for it," she says.

CHAPTER 2

Desert and More

TAKE A LOOK AT LIBYA ON A MAP OF AFRICA. Usually you'll see a vast stretch of tan—it's almost all desert. About 90 percent of Libya is part of the Sahara, the largest desert in the world, which spreads across the northern third of Africa. But Libya is more than just desert.

Libya's northern border is a coastline. It stretches for about 1,100 miles (1,770 kilometers) along the Mediterranean Sea. A great majority of Libya's population—about 85 percent—

Opposite: **Palm trees grow around Mandara Lakes, at an oasis in southwestern Libya.**

Libya's Geographic Features

Area: 679,362 square miles (1,759,540 sq km)

Greatest Distance North to South: 930 miles (1,500 km)

Greatest Distance East to West: 1,050 miles (1,700 km)

Highest Elevation: Bikku Bitti, 7,438 feet (2,267 m) above sea level

Lowest Elevation: Sabkhat Ghuzayyil, 154 feet (47 m) below sea level

Longest Known Cave: Umm al-Masabih, 2.2 miles (3.5 km) long

Length of Coastline: 1,100 miles (1,770 km)

Average Annual Precipitation: About 15 inches (38 cm) in Tripoli; less than 1 inch (2.5 cm) in the Sahara

Average High Temperature: In Tripoli, 64°F (17.5°C) in January, 96°F (36°C) in July; in Sabha, 65°F (18°C) in January, 102°F (39°C) in July

Average Low Temperature: In Tripoli, 45°F (7°C) in January, 70°F (21°C) in July; in Sabha, 43°F (6°C) in January, 76°F (25°C) in July

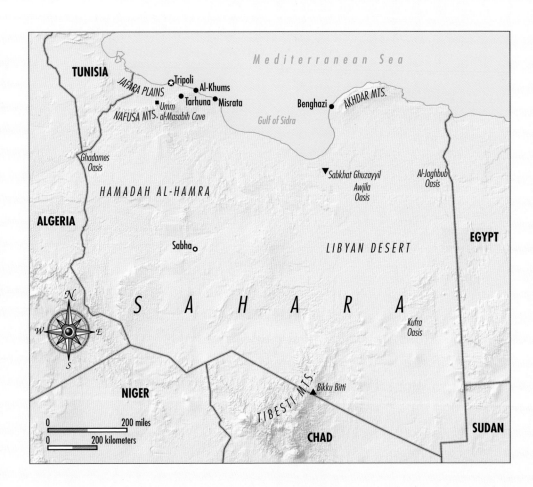

lives along the coast. In addition to cities, the coastal region also includes lush green fields, marshes, lagoons, and brilliant, sun-drenched beaches. Elsewhere in the country, high, rugged mountains rise.

Libya is Africa's fourth-largest country, covering 679,362 square miles (1,759,540 sq km) of land. Only Algeria, Democratic Republic of Congo, and Sudan are larger. Libya is roughly the size of the U.S. state of Alaska.

Libya has historically been divided into three regions—Tripolitania, Fezzan, and Cyrenaica—each with its own distinct characteristics.

Libya's warm Mediterranean coastline features both sandy beaches and dramatic rocky shores.

Tripolitania

Tripolitania covers northwestern Libya from the border with Tunisia to the Gulf of Sidra, a large indent along the Libyan coastline. The region spreads inland for several hundred miles. The city of Tripoli, Libya's capital and largest city, is located on the coast in this area of Tripolitania. Nearly one-third of Libya's people live in and around Tripoli.

Tripolitania includes a stretch of low-lying land that runs along the coast of the Mediterranean Sea. This strip, about 6 miles (10 km) wide and 185 miles (300 km) long, abounds with sand flats and marshy lagoons.

A Look at Libya's Cities

The largest city in Libya is its capital, Tripoli, which has more than 1.1 million residents. The second-largest is Benghazi (below right), home to some 650,000 people. Benghazi lies in northeastern Libya on the Mediterranean Sea. Founded by Greeks in about 515 BCE, Benghazi was once a jewel of a city. When it was rebuilt after damage suffered during World War II, it was described as a gleaming showpiece of modern Libya. It was a center of oil refining and a busy seaport with impressive shops and lively beaches. But it became a sight of major violence during the uprising of 2011. Today, it suffers from severe economic problems and ongoing armed conflict.

Misrata, too, has fallen on hard times. The third-largest city in Libya with about 386,000 residents, it is located east of Tripoli in northeastern Libya. The city was founded in about 800 BCE as a supply center for caravans and has been a trading center ever since. Today, it boasts the nation's best port and is strong economically. Groves of palm and olive trees surround the city.

Tarhuna and Al-Khums are Libya's fourth- and fifth-largest cities, each with just over 200,000 residents. Though they still feel the economic pain that's common in all of Libya, both have escaped the violence and fighting better than other large cities. Tarhuna is located southeast of Tripoli. It is a major center for agriculture, producing olive oil, cereals, figs, grapes, and nuts. Al-Khums (above) is in the same area though nearer the coast. Tourism has been an important part of this city's economy, as it is near the ancient Roman city of Leptis Magna.

Almond trees grow well in the dry soil near Tripoli.

Agriculture is important along the coast. Fields of wheat, barley, soybeans, cauliflower, peanuts, and tomatoes supply produce for the large population. Groves of trees produce dates, almonds, olives, and citrus fruits.

Farther south, Tripolitania features large stretches of coarse grasslands. These are laced with *wadis*—riverbeds that are dry most of the year. During the rainy season, however, wadis fill with water that rushes to the sea.

Inland, the land rises to merge with the Jafara Plains. These broad, flat plains are desertlike, with only a few scrubby plants growing here and there. Farther south still is the Nafusa mountain range. These striking mountains rise abruptly from the coastal plain. Old craters and rock made from lava indicate that these mountains were formed by volcanic activity. The Nafusa Mountains, which reach elevations of about 3,000 feet (900 meters), are mostly bare except for a few fig trees.

South of the Nafusas, the land levels out into the Hamadah al-Hamra, also known as the Red Desert. Its name comes from the red sandstone at its base. The Red Desert is huge, stretching for hundreds of miles with little visible but sand and gravel.

A young man stands on a towering rock in Tarmeisa village, high in the Nafusa Mountains.

A forest of rock formations rises from the red sand in the Libyan Desert.

Fezzan

Fezzan is a desert area that makes up most of southwestern Libya. In Fezzan, vast sand dunes—some several hundred feet high—change shape slowly with the shifting wind. These dunes cover about one-fifth of Fezzan. Much of the rest of the region is jagged, rocky plateau. The wind and intense temperature changes of the desert sculpt some of the rocks into odd shapes.

Most of Fezzan is fairly flat, but the Tibesti Mountains rise in the south along the border with Chad. These mountains include Bikku Bitti, the highest point in Libya with an elevation of 7,438 feet (2,267 m) above sea level.

In some places in Fezzan, underground water reaches the dry land on the earth's surface, creating an oasis. An oasis is a

From Jungle to Desert

At least fourteen thousand years ago, people began carving pictures into the rocks in the land now called Libya. These ancient pictures tell of a time when the environment was very different from what it is today. The rock art shows large lakes and flowing rivers. Grasses, shrubs, and trees grow nearby. Large herds of animals roam the land. There are drawings of crocodiles, elephants, giraffes, hippopotamuses, ostriches, and zebras.

Fossils confirm what these drawings depict. Libya was once a lush, tropical place. For about 4,500 years, ending around 5,500 years ago, most of North Africa was covered with fertile grasslands and jungles.

But why is it mostly desert today? To find out, some scientists have used computers to model Earth's climate from thousands of years ago. Others have taken samples from the bottom of the Atlantic Ocean. These samples contain sand and dirt blown west from Africa over the course of thirty thousand years. Both the climate models and the ocean samples indicate that the change from jungle to desert happened quickly. In the course of just three hundred years, rivers and lakes dried up, plants disappeared, and animals moved south. The great Sahara Desert began to form. This abrupt change is considered one of the most striking environmental transformations in history.

Most scientists now believe that these changes resulted from a tiny shift in Earth's orbit. The gravitational pull from other bodies in the solar system caused Earth to wobble a bit. About eight thousand years ago, Earth was tilted 24.1 degrees on its axis. Today, its tilt is 23.5 degrees. That slight shift was enough to lessen the amount of sunlight that hit the Northern Hemisphere. The additional sunlight had once added heat, strength-

ening monsoons, winds that carry water in from the ocean. With less sunlight, there were fewer monsoons. Without enough water, plants began to disappear.

Having fewer plants intensified the problem because plants hold the moisture from the rain that falls and then release it back into the atmosphere. So, with fewer plants, there was less moisture in the atmosphere and less rain falling. The cycle continued, and the region dried up. The Sahara Desert was born.

Small trees, bushes, and grasses cover the Green Mountains in eastern Libya.

patch of green in the sandy desert. Its deep underground wells or springs provide enough water for trees, grass, and shrubs to grow. Some large oases support villages, while smaller oases may serve as the home of only one or two families.

Cyrenaica

Libya's largest geographical region is Cyrenaica. Located in the eastern part of the country, it covers nearly half the land. It includes Libya's eastern Mediterranean coast, a rich agricultural area that supports vineyards and fruit orchards. Cyrenaica also includes three important port cities along the coast here: Benghazi, Derna, and Tobruk.

Away from the coast, the land rises steeply about 2,900 feet (880 m) to a rocky plateau called the Akhdar Mountains, or Green Mountains. The flowers that cover the lower slopes are what give it its name. Anemones, cyclamens, lilies, and narcissi all add beautiful color. At higher elevations there are shrubs and junipers. The Akhdar Mountains extend south all the way to the Libyan Desert, a part of the Sahara.

Some sections of the Libyan Desert are bare and rocky. Other parts are sandy. But nearly all of it is inhospitable. People don't live there. The few oases in the desert are the only exception to this. Kufra is one of the largest oases in the nation.

Circles of Green

Even if you were an astronaut orbiting Earth, you'd be able to see the Kufra Oasis in Libya. It is one of the most easily recognizable features on Earth from the International Space Station. Astronauts can pick out the large circles of green that form neat rows in the midst of

the vast Sahara. The circles show where central pivot irrigation is in use. In the center of each circle is a well, drilled deep into the underground water supply. The water is pumped up into a series of sprinklers that rotate around the well in a circular pattern. Each one of these circles is larger than a half mile (1 km) across. Dates, as well as other fruits and vegetables, are grown in Kufra. Farmers in the oasis also grow grain to feed livestock.

The oasis itself is about 30 miles (48 km) long and 12 miles (19 km) wide. The water that feeds the oasis settled in large pools underground about ten thousand years ago. At that time, the region had rivers and lakes and received plentiful rainfall. Some of this water seeped underground through the porous sandstone and has been held there ever since. In some places it is more than 2 miles (3 km) below the surface.

Long ago, Kufra grew as a stop on caravan routes across the desert. Today, the oasis has three main towns, with a total population of about sixty thousand.

Libya's strong winds sometimes whip up sandstorms. The storms can damage car engines and other machinery.

Climate

More than 90 percent of Libya is desert, so it's no surprise that the country is hot and dry. Daytime summer temperatures in the Sahara average almost 100 degrees Fahrenheit (38 degrees Celsius) and often reach 115°F (46°C). It's cooler in the winter, with temperatures of only 60 or 70°F (16 or 21°C). In the high mountain ranges along Libya's southern border, it is even cooler. Sometimes, it actually snows there.

Only a small amount of rain falls in the desert. Some parts of the desert receive an average of 4 inches (10 centimeters) per year, while others receive as little as 0.2 inches (0.5 cm) in some years. In the spring and fall, winds from the desert carry swirls of dust and sand all the way north to the Mediterranean

Sea. These hot winds, called *ghiblis*, usually last one to four days. They can damage crops along the coast in the spring. In the fall, the warm winds are welcome, since they help the date crops ripen faster.

The Mediterranean Sea affects weather in Libya's coastal areas. Summers are hot and humid. Winters are much cooler, and most of the year's 14 to 22 inches (36 to 56 cm) of rain falls then. Farther south, the plains region of Cyrenaica gets the heaviest rainfall in Libya—about 26 inches (66 cm) each year. These rains often cause flash floods because the parched ground does not absorb moisture easily.

Although the desert is often hot during the day, at night the temperature drops quickly. In the winter, the temperature is often near freezing at night.

Water

There are no rivers in Libya that flow year-round. Instead, it has *wadis*, rivers that form during the rainy season following heavy downpours.

Libya borders the Mediterranean Sea, but water for agriculture is in short supply. Seawater can't be used to grow crops because as it evaporates it leaves behind a layer of salt, which damages the soil and plants. Many of the wells that supplied

Salt encrusts the land in an area of Libya where water has evaporated.

Floodwaters trap vehicles during a storm in Libya in 2015.

fresh water to Libya's farms for centuries are nearly dry. Others have become too salty to use as seawater seeps into them.

The Great Man-Made River (GMR) is a huge project meant to help solve Libya's water problems. Begun in 1984, the GMR taps into large reserves of fresh water under the desert in the southern part of the country. The water has been there, trapped between layers of rock and sand, for about thirty thousand years. Some 1,300 wells have been drilled in the region, and more than 3,000 miles (5,000 km) of water pipeline stretch across the nation. These concrete pipes are

Children play in a lake created by the opening of the Great Man-Made River.

large enough to drive a truck through. The GMR was supposed to supply 1.7 billion gallons (6.4 million cubic meters) of water each day to farms and cities in the northern portions of Libya.

By 2011, the GMR project was nearly complete. Benghazi and other thirsty cities in northern Libya were receiving fresh water. But during the revolt that ousted Libya's leader Muammar Qaddafi, North Atlantic Treaty Organization (NATO) forces helping the rebels bombed the GMR. They also struck the factory in Brega, Libya, where the large concrete pipes were made. NATO officials explained that weapons were being transported in the river tunnels, and that factories were actually hiding rocket launchers used by Qaddafi's forces to attack civilians.

Following the bombing, nearly half of Libya's residents were without running water. Some has been restored. But because of the ongoing turmoil, the electricity needed to pump the water through the tunnels is sometimes disrupted, so water from the GMR is not always available for the people of Libya.

Women in Tripoli gather water bottles that they will fill and distribute to people in need. The recent violence has disrupted the water supply to some parts of the nation.

CHAPTER 3

Adapting to the Desert

LIBYA IS HOME TO A WIDE VARIETY OF PLANTS AND animals that live in many different environments. There are many kinds of life-forms in the coastal regions and oases, where food and water is plentiful for fish, birds, and mammals. But some survive in harsher regions.

Plants and animals that live in the desert must be able to survive in extreme heat and with little water. They have adapted to be able to thrive in this challenging environment in a variety of different ways.

Opposite: **The fennec fox is well adapted to life in the desert. It stays in its underground den during the heat of the day and comes out at night to hunt.**

Camels feed on grasses in the Libyan Desert. A camel's hump is made of fat, which it can draw on for nourishment when food is not available.

Mammals

When most people think of desert animals, they think of camels. Camels are particularly well-suited to lives in the sand and heat. They can live for more than a week without water. After going without water for several days, a camel can drink as much as 25 gallons of water (95 liters) at one time. Camels have many other adaptations that help them survive in the desert. They can close their eyes and nostrils so tightly during a windstorm that not a speck of sand blows in. They can survive eating nothing but thorny desert shrubs and the pits of dates. The big, wide, leathery soles of their feet keep camels from sinking into the sand and also help them walk across rocky ground. And camels can smell water from as far away as 1 mile (1.6 km)!

Ships of the Desert

Camels arrived in North Africa about two thousand years ago when Persians brought them to Egypt from Asia. Within one hundred years, camels were common throughout the Sahara. They are sometimes called the "ships of the desert" because just as people relied on ships to carry them across the vast oceans, they relied on camels to carry them safely across the desert.

For centuries, desert people found camels to be vital to their survival. They used camels to carry their goods, since camels can carry as much as 1,000 pounds (450 kilograms) at a time. Camel's milk is good to drink, and it can be used to make cheese. The hair from their bellies can be woven into soft cloth, strong enough to make tents. Even their droppings have a purpose—when dried, these are good fuel for fires.

In modern times, camels are seldom used for travel; today, people travel across the desert in jeeps. But the camel remains a beloved and important symbol of Libya's history.

Other mammals have different adaptations that help them survive the challenging conditions of Libya's hot Saharan desert. One method is estivation, which means staying inactive during the hot months of summer. It is similar to how many animals survive by hibernating, or sleeping through cold winters. Many desert rodents practice estivation. Some birds such as nighthawks do, too, though it is more common among mammals.

Other Libyan animals, such as jerboas, are nocturnal. This means they sleep during the day and come out at night, when it is cooler. Jerboas are rodents, the size of mice but with long,

Barbary sheep race across the desert. The animals typically live in small family groups.

powerful hind legs that propel them forward. Their long tails help them balance as they hop, sort of like a tiny kangaroo, as far as 10 feet (3 m) at a time.

The jerboa stays under the sand when temperatures soar during the day, and emerges to feed on desert plants and insects at night. It does not drink any water, since it gets all the water it needs from the food it eats.

Most of Libya's desert mammals have sand-colored fur. This trait helps them in two ways. First, it makes it more difficult for predators to find them because their coloring blends in with the background of sand and rocks. This is called camouflage, having a body that naturally blends in with the landscape. Secondly, their light coloring reflects heat from the sun, helping the animals stay cooler in the scorching desert.

Barbary sheep, for example, have this trait. Their colors

blend in with the light sandy tones of Libya's desert mountains. The sheep are most active at night. During the day they tend to rest in shade. Their diet contains a wide variety of grasses, leaves, small shrubs, and flowers. These plants contain a good deal of water, so the sheep can go for several days without drinking water if they need to. When they find a water source, though, they take full advantage of it. They usually drink a lot and even play in the water.

Fennec foxes, too, are tan. They also have exceptionally large ears that help keep them cool because the heat can escape their bodies through their ears. They get all the water they need to survive by eating other desert animals—especially jerboas.

The National Animal

Barbary lions once roamed the mountains and deserts of Libya. Though they are now extinct, they remain Libya's national animal. Larger than most other lions, Barbary lions also had a darker mane. Several royal families of African nations held large numbers of them in captivity. Many Europeans, who encountered Barbary lions when they controlled Libya and other parts of North Africa, also admired the creatures. Huge packs of them were taken to Rome, Italy, where they battled gladiators in front of huge crowds, and many were put on display in zoos. Thousands of the lions died. More were killed when European hunters traveled to Africa to shoot them for sport. By the early twentieth century, they were nearly extinct, and a French hunter killed the last Barbary lion in the wild in 1922.

Reptiles

Several types of lizards and poisonous snakes live in Libya's deserts. Reptiles are cold-blooded, meaning their temperature changes with their surroundings. At night their bodies become chilled, so in the morning they lie in the sun to get warm before sneaking back under the sand. Skinks are a common lizard in Libya. They have jaws shaped like a wedge, which they use to dig holes in the cool sand where they will rest. A layer of transparent scales protects their eyes.

Snakes in Libya include Cleopatra's asp, several types of adders, and the horned viper. These snakes are colored like sand and pebbles, so they blend in well with the rocky desert. Kraits are another snake of the Libyan desert. They are brightly colored and would stand out against the dull sand and rocks during the light of day, so they hunt in the dark of night, when they can slither up to unsuspecting victims, mostly other snakes and small mammals, and sink their grooved fangs into them.

Birds

Desert birds include vultures and hawks. Another bird of the Libyan desert, the sand grouse, has an unusual adaptation for life in a dry desert climate. Most birds have feathers that repel water, but the sand grouse's feathers absorb water. This way, adult birds can carry moisture back to their nests to cool their eggs.

The red kite is one of the largest birds of prey found in Libya. They usually feed on small animals such as mice.

Date palms are one of the most popular fruit trees in Libya. A bunch can include more than a thousand dates.

Many more types of birds live along the coast. Bright pink flamingos gather along beaches and lakes. Plovers, storks, herons, and ducks are also found at beaches and lagoons.

Plant Life

Plants have also developed adaptations that help them survive in the desert. Most desert plants have long root systems that tap into groundwater far below the surface. They have small leaves so that very little moisture is able to evaporate.

Date palm trees grow wild in oases. They are hardy trees and useful in many ways. Dates are a delicious fruit eaten fresh or dried. Their seeds can be ground and mixed with flour, and their sweet juice makes a treat that tastes something like honey. Palm tree trunks are used for lumber and fuel, and the palm fronds are woven into sandals, baskets, and mats. People use every part of the date palm.

Cactuses are also common in Libyan oases. Many Libyans enjoy eating the sweet, juicy fruit of the prickly pear cactus. Wild pistachios are another popular food from the oases.

Grass grows in most nondesert areas of Libya. Esparto grass, which is used for making paper and rope, was at one time Libya's chief export. Leaves from the henna plant are used to make red dye. Some Libyan women dye their hair with henna or use it to paint intricate designs on their hands.

The coastal region has the most abundant plant life. There, plants such as asphodel, a relative of the lily, grow wild. In the Akhdar Mountains of the northeast, trees such as juniper flourish.

Typically, the desert looks mostly barren. But every ten years or so when heavy rains fall, Libya's desert blossoms! The seeds and bulbs that produce the greenery can survive long, dry periods. Then, as soon as they get water, they grow into plants. Flowers display vivid colors, along with the green of grasses and herbs.

National Flower

The pomegranate blossom is Libya's national flower. Its delicate, reddish-pink petals bloom on the fruit trees, which usually grow to a height of 16 to 26 feet (5 to 8 m). These trees have been cultivated in Libya and throughout the Mediterranean region since ancient times. They thrive in dry climates.

CHAPTER 4

The Story of Libya

P EOPLE HAVE LIVED IN NORTH AFRICA FOR TENS of thousands of years. Much of North Africa was once lush and bountiful. But the region dried out about 5,500 years ago, and the Sahara expanded. As the climate and plant life in the region changed, so did human lives. People could no longer rely on bountiful nature to provide them with the food they needed. Some people on the coastal plain settled there to become farmers. The coastal people were good at raising animals and growing crops. They lived this way, in small groups, for about two thousand years.

Opposite: **Prehistoric rock paintings in southern Libya depict the people who once lived in the region and the animals they hunted.**

Over time, other people migrated into the area from the east, and the people of the region came to be called Berbers. The origin of the term *Berber* is not certain, but it likely came from the word *barbarian*, which was used to mean people who spoke a language other than Greek or Latin. The Berber people call themselves Imazighen, a term that means "the free people."

The people of Libya became successful farmers and flourished. Because their fertile land was valuable, outsiders eventually fought to control the Mediterranean coast.

Phoenician trading ships had large square sails. The sailors used long, oar-like blades to help steer.

Outsiders Arrive

Phoenician sailors came from the land that is now Lebanon in the eastern Mediterranean. They built shipping ports in the Tripolitania region beginning in 1300 BCE. The Phoenicians' main concern was creating a place to anchor their ships along their trade route from Phoenicia to Spain. They wanted to make sure that the water passage remained open to them. They depended on their homeland for supplies, so they didn't travel farther inland to search for resources. Nor did they establish new communities in Libya.

However, Phoenicians also settled farther west along the coast, in what is now Tunisia. There, they founded the city of Carthage. It became a wealthy seaport and an independent power in its own right. Carthage developed a strong military force, which eventually ruled much of the North African coast, including Tripolitania.

The Carthaginians established colonies in Tripolitania and Cyrenaica. They were not kind to the Berbers who lived there. Carthaginians forced the strongest Berber men into their military. Other Berbers were put to work farming. The Carthaginian rulers demanded as much as half the Berbers' crops each season.

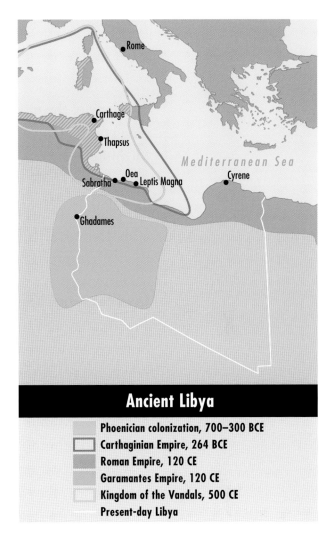

Ancient Libya

Phoenician colonization, 700–300 BCE
Carthaginian Empire, 264 BCE
Roman Empire, 120 CE
Garamantes Empire, 120 CE
Kingdom of the Vandals, 500 CE
Present-day Libya

Many of the most prosperous Carthaginian cities were stopping points along a trade route across the Sahara. It linked the Mediterranean Sea with the Niger River. Along that route, dealers from many lands exchanged slaves as well as gemstones, fine cloth, foods, spices, and other goods. But over time, wars and lack of resources slowed down the traffic across the Sahara. As the trade route faded, so did the Carthaginian cities.

Invaders and Empires

The next groups to rule the region were the Greeks and the Romans, and both established powerful cities in what is now Libya. Some of the monuments they built remain standing today. In 146 BCE, Romans took over the Carthaginian Empire. The farms in Tripolitania became the main sources of grains and other foods for the Roman Empire.

Greeks took hold in Cyrenaica and developed a fishing port. At first, they were successful. But as more Greeks moved in to share the wealth, those already living there began to rebel. Control of the land changed hands many times. Because there was no strong local organization, Romans saw an opportunity to take over. Eventually, Cyrenaica also fell under Roman rule.

For several hundred years, the area prospered and the population grew. Leptis Magna was a Roman city that arose on the site of an ancient Phoenician city. By 200 CE, it was the largest city in Libya, with about eighty thousand residents. In Tripoli, the Romans built a white marble arch in 163 CE honoring Marcus Aurelius, the emperor of Rome. At the time, the

Roman Empire was in decline, but Marcus restored much of the empire's glory. He made sure that it had a strong military to protect it from invaders.

But once again the empire began to collapse and Romans lost control of North Africa. The Vandals, a group from what is now Germany, arrived in about 435 CE. The Vandals fought for control of Roman shipyards, grain supplies, and other valuable resources. Along the way, they looted and ransacked buildings and artwork. Their name gave rise to the term *vandalism*, meaning senseless destruction. The Vandals controlled much of the coastal region for more than a century.

Farther inland, the Garamantes ruled the Fezzan for fifteen centuries, starting in 1000 BCE. They controlled much of the trade route across the Sahara. Along this route, ivory and gold

Leptis Magna is considered one of the finest Roman ruins in the world. The remarkable remains include markets, baths, temples, and theaters.

Preserving History

Recent fighting in Libya has damaged some of its most important historic sites. The United Nations Educational, Scientific and Cultural Organization (UNESCO) is an organization that chooses cultural and natural sites around the world for preservation. These are called World Heritage sites because they have unusual importance to humanity. In 2016, all five World Heritage Sites in Libya were placed on UNESCO's list of locations in danger.

A site called Cyrene has fared the worst. It is the remains of an ancient Greek colony. It included a shrine that the Romans later enlarged and turned into an amphitheater where trained fighters called gladiators battled wild animals. Other monuments at Cyrene include the Temple of Apollo and the Sanctuary of Zeus. Cyrene has suffered irreversible damage. Illegal construction has taken place at the site, and bulldozers have vandalized ancient tombs.

Other sites have suffered less damage but are in danger because they are near combat zones. One of these is Sabratha (below), which was a flourishing Phoenician port city during the second and third centuries CE. The site includes a beautiful theater surrounded on three sides by pink and white marble walls.

Ghadames (above) was once an important city in the ancient Garamantes Empire, which was based in the Fezzan. People have lived on this site for many thousands of years. Inside its walled city are clusters of multistory homes made of clay and brick. The tranquil oasis settlement today sits in a volatile area.

Leptis Magna was one of the grandest cities in the Roman world, with a beautiful harbor and ornate marble and granite buildings. After suffering several attacks, the city fell into ruin and was largely abandoned in the 600s. Sand eventually buried it. Leptis Magna was not uncovered until the early twentieth century. Today, the ruins of houses, a market, a church, and other buildings have been uncovered.

Tadrart Acacus, a desert site in western Libya, features thousands of paintings and carvings on rock. Some of this art is twelve thousand years old. This art shows the plants, animals, and human activity that existed at the time it was made. Even before the fighting in Libya, some visitors and photographers damaged the site by wetting the drawings to make them stand out better.

UNESCO has taken several steps to help secure these sites. Heritage police help keep out vandals, and important historical objects have been hidden.

from deep in Africa were carried north to the Mediterranean Sea. Pyramid tombs built by the Garamantes still stand today.

Arab Invasion

Libya's history took a dramatic turn in 643 CE, the year Arabs arrived in the region. They came from the Arabian Peninsula, the part of Asia that lies just to the east of Africa. The Arabs brought with them the new religion of Islam. Founded in 622, the faith was rapidly spreading throughout the Middle East and North Africa. Many people in what is now Libya quickly adopted Islam.

Some walls still stand in the ancient Garamantes city of Germa.

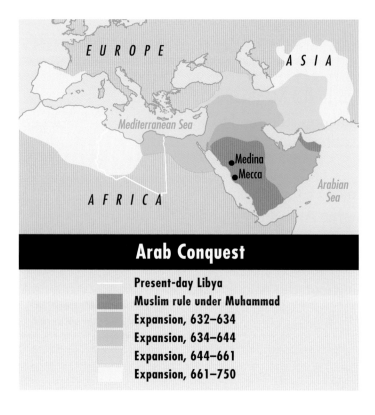

Arab Conquest

- Present-day Libya
- Muslim rule under Muhammad
- Expansion, 632–634
- Expansion, 634–644
- Expansion, 644–661
- Expansion, 661–750

EUROPE

ASIA

Mediterranean Sea

Medina
Mecca

Arabian
Sea

AFRICA

In the eleventh century, large groups of Arabs arrived in North Africa to help maintain control of the region. Thousands of families came to North Africa from Egypt. They spread throughout Tripolitania, Cyrenaica, and the Fezzan. Arab culture quickly took hold. In just four hundred years, Islam had become the dominant religion in Libya.

Today, 97 percent of Libyans are Muslim, and the Arabic language is dominant throughout the country. Most Libyans today claim Arab heritage, along with their Berber roots. No other group of invaders left their mark on Libya as permanently as Arabs did.

Invasions and Empires

In the centuries that followed, invaders continued to arrive. Normans from Europe took over Tripoli in 1146. Later, the Almohads, a Muslim group from Morocco, ruled for more than two hundred years. They were followed by Spaniards, who arrived in 1510. Four decades later came the Ottoman Turks, and Libya became part of the Ottoman Empire.

The Ottomans were not a colonizing force. Instead, they held some control over the region and demanded taxes. Libya was part of the Ottoman Empire for more than three hundred years.

The Barbary Pirates

In the late 1700s, a fearsome group of sailors controlled parts of the Mediterranean Sea. They were called the Barbary pirates after their Berber heritage. Their main port was Tripoli. They raided ships, including American merchant vessels. The pirates stole goods and kidnapped and enslaved crew members, sometimes holding them for ransom. At one point, Barbary pirates held more than thirty thousand captives, hoping to collect ransom money for them. The pirates also demanded money from foreign nations in return for allowing their ships to travel through the Mediterranean without harassment. These payments were called tribute.

Beginning in 1795, the United States paid the pirates a yearly tribute of more than US$2 million. In 1801, when the pirate leaders demanded even higher payments, the United States refused and fighting broke out. The U.S. Navy was created to battle these pirates. The "Marines' Hymn," the official song of the U.S. Marine Corps, mentions this origin of the U.S. Navy in its opening lines: "From the halls of Montezuma,/To the shores of Tripoli."

The U.S. Navy defeated the Barbary pirates in a battle at Tripoli in 1805. The peace was only temporary, however. Fighting began again in 1812 and lasted for several more years until the pirates' power weakened and the strength of the United States grew.

The Sanusi Brotherhood

In time, a group in Libya called the Sanusi Brotherhood emerged. This organization would eventually become vital in the movement for Libyan independence.

The Sanusi Brotherhood was formed in 1837 by an Algerian named Sidi Muhammad ibn-Ali al-Sanusi. He established the group to help return to the simple beliefs and lifestyle of early Islam. Many members were missionaries, who helped spread Islam farther throughout North Africa.

Tripoli in the 1850s. The city's good harbor made it desirable to invaders.

Sanusi took his ideas to Cyrenaica. Members of the brotherhood pledged their loyalty to him. They established lodges, called *zawiyas*, throughout Cyrenaica and in parts of Tripolitania. The zawiyas were places to gather. Members received spiritual guidance and planned political moves. As the Sanusi Brotherhood became more powerful locally, it drew the attention of the Ottomans. The two groups cooperated, but the Ottoman Empire was weakening. Finally, around 1910, the Italians moved in.

Italian Rule

Italian rule was very different from Ottoman rule. The Italians wanted to colonize and control Libya. They were interested in Libya for several reasons. Control of Tripoli would give

Italy greater shipping power in the Mediterranean Sea. Italy also wanted a presence in North Africa. The British already controlled Egypt, and the Italians feared that France wanted Libya. After months of fighting against the invading Italian forces, the Ottomans gave up their rights to Libya in 1912.

Italians declared that Libya was rightfully theirs, since the remains of the cities built by their Roman ancestors hundreds of years earlier still stood there. But Tripolitania was the only region the Italians managed to control. When Italy entered

Italian forces lead Libyan prisoners through Tripoli in 1911.

A Symbol of Resistance

Omar al-Mukhtar (1862–1931) was a teacher and Qur'an scholar who loved studying. But he became a man of action when he could no longer tolerate Italian rule. He pulled together the mujahideen, a resistance movement that nearly forced the Italians from Libya.

Al-Mukhtar became known as the Mentor of Bravery for his fearless leadership of the mujahideen. He skillfully tracked the movements of the Italians and used his knowledge of the Libyan landscape to ambush them.

Al-Mukhtar had led the mujahideen for nearly twenty years when he was wounded in battle and captured in 1931. The Italians shackled him in chains, convicted him, and then hanged him on September 16, 1931, in front of thousands of mourning Libyans. Today, al-Mukhtar is honored as one of Libya's greatest heroes.

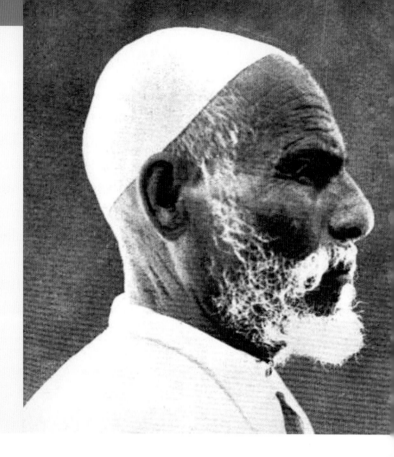

World War I in 1915, the attention of the Italians turned elsewhere. They had to focus on the war.

In Cyrenaica, a teacher named Omar al-Mukhtar formed a resistance group. Mukhtar's resistance movement was based on the networks of the Sanusi Brotherhood. His forces called themselves the mujahideen, or "freedom fighters." With good horses but old military equipment, they battled tens of thousands of Italian troops. Though they weren't successful, the mujahideen almost defeated the Italians. The Italians executed al-Mukhtar. He became an important figure in history, representing the struggle for freedom.

At the end of World War I, Italy again focused on colonizing the Libyan region. The Italian effort to subdue Libya was brutal. They murdered civilians, and there were instances when they threw prisoners from airplanes or ran them over with tanks. In 1931, Italy announced that it had control of the region.

Finally Free

Libya was freed from Italian rule in 1943, when Italy was defeated in World War II. After the war, the United Nations decided that Libya should become a constitutional monarchy. Under this system of government, a king or queen rules but has powers limited by a constitution.

Italian colonists arrive in Tripoli in 1938. Italy made a strong effort to colonize Libya, sending poor Italians to the region and often giving them land taken from Libyans. By 1939, more than 12 percent of the people in Libya were Italian.

King Idris greets crowds of Libyans on December 24, 1951, the day Libya became independent.

The country became independent in 1951. Muhammad Idris al-Sanusi, who had led the fight against Italy, was chosen to be the first king. But he was a weak leader. Most of his support came from his home region of Cyrenaica, even though most of the population lived in and around Tripoli, the capital. Idris tried to increase his power by breaking the law. He shut down political parties so that those who disagreed with him could not gain support.

Libya had other problems as well. The nation was poor. Most people made their living by farming, selling a few small items in villages, or hunting and gathering what they could in the desert. Libya, in the early 1950s, was one of the poorest nations in the world. But things were about to change rapidly.

Oil!

In June 1959, joyful cheers rang out in the Libyan Desert in Cyrenaica. Oil! Major reserves were found by the American company Esso, which later became Exxon. Libya was on its way to becoming a major economic force. More oil was soon discovered, and the country quickly began exporting it.

In the 1960s, long pipelines were laid to carry oil from the desert to the coast, where it could be shipped to other countries.

In the 1960s, Tripoli was a thriving city, home to about two hundred thousand people.

The oil strikes came at a good time. People around the world were driving more and more cars in the early 1960s, and they needed oil to fuel them. As the demand for oil increased, the price of oil went up, and Libya got richer. People got jobs. The country expanded its military. Schools and hospitals, roads and houses were built. Communication systems improved.

Still, most of the oil money stayed in the hands of government and business leaders. Most Libyans lived the same difficult lives as they had before oil was discovered. Though more goods and services were available in the country, the cost of living went up. Ordinary people still could not get ahead.

By the late 1960s, King Idris was growing old. His government was wracked by corruption. Many Libyans were upset. When the king left the country for medical treatment in 1969, a rebel military group saw its chance. It took over the king's palace and the nation's military bases. The rebels locked up supporters of the king. The leader of the rebel group, Muammar Qaddafi, went on the radio to tell the people of Libya that he had overthrown their government. Only twenty-seven years old, Qaddafi was the new leader of Libya. King Idris never returned to Libya. He died in Cairo, Egypt, in 1983.

Muammar Qaddafi

Muammar Qaddafi was an unlikely leader. He was from a poor family of Bedouin, nomadic people who raised goats and moved about the Libyan Desert. As a child, he lived in a home made of goatskin.

Qaddafi was smart, and he stood out. His parents saw his abilities and scraped together enough money to send him to a boarding school. There, most of his classmates came from wealthy families. Their fathers were businesspeople, and their families had left the traditional ways behind.

Qaddafi was an outsider. He was devoted to his Muslim faith, and had no interest in the lifestyles of his classmates. He focused on his schoolwork. Quickly he moved to the top of his class. When he was lonely he would listen to the radio. He especially enjoyed programs that featured speeches by Gamal Abdel Nasser, who was then president of Egypt. Nasser often talked about his desire to see Arab nations work together. He wanted them to have strong ties to their Muslim faith and traditional culture. Qaddafi took this message to heart.

At a different school, Qaddafi met more children from poor families who agreed with his ideas about the direction the country should take. Soon Qaddafi had a large but secretive following. He and his supporters began to plot ways to get rid of King Idris. These plans continued to develop as Qaddafi went on to the University of Libya, the Libyan Military College, and a career in the Libyan army. In 1969, all his ideas came together. At age twenty-seven, Qaddafi led the rebel group that stormed the king's palace and took control of Libya.

The Lockerbie Bombing

A low point in Libya's relations with the United States came in 1988, when a plane traveling from London to New York blew up over Lockerbie, Scotland. All 259 people on board were killed, along with another 11 people on the ground. After years of studying the rubble and other information, investigators linked the crash to two Libyan intelligence officers who planted a bomb on board.

Libya refused to turn the two men over so they could be tried. In response, the United Nations imposed trade restrictions on Libya. These restrictions hurt Libya's economy badly, but they did not sway Qaddafi. Mainly, it was the general public in Libya who felt the pain from the trade restrictions. Finally, in 1999, Libya turned over the suspects, who were tried in Europe. One was cleared

of murder charges and another was sentenced to twenty-seven years in prison. In 2003, Libya paid money to the families of those killed in the Lockerbie bombing.

Once Qaddafi took power, changes happened quickly. He renamed the country the Libyan Arab Republic and shut down all the agencies of the old government. Qaddafi remained in charge for forty-two years. During that time, Libya faced many challenges.

First, Qaddafi stirred up difficult relationships with other nations. He wanted to unite the Arab world, a notion he'd taken from President Gamal Abdel Nasser of Egypt. Qaddafi felt Libya should be a major power in this Arab union and met with many leaders to encourage this plan. But it was ultimately unsuccessful. Many Arab leaders found Qaddafi too aggressive, and Libya had poor relations with most of its neighboring countries. It fought a border war with Chad for more than twenty years and had tense relations with other North African and Arab nations, including Egypt, Morocco, Sudan, Tunisia, and Syria.

Libya's relationship with the Western world, especially the United States, was also tense throughout Qaddafi's time in office. Many people were concerned that he wanted to destroy the Jewish state of Israel. Qaddafi and Libya were responsible for several acts of terrorism around the world, beginning in the 1970s.

The United States responded by placing trade restrictions on Libya, in an attempt to hurt the Libyan economy, especially the oil industry. The United States also shot down two Libyan planes and bombed what it said were terrorist training sites in Tripoli and Benghazi. Dozens of Libyan civilians were killed.

By the late 1990s, Qaddafi began to work more closely with other nations, both in Africa and around the world. Relations with the United States and other Western nations improved. In return, sanctions were dropped. Libya was removed from the United States' list of nations that support terrorism. Libya, Qaddafi said in 2007, is "determined to participate in a new world of peace, liberty, and cooperation among nations and civilizations." This would not come to pass.

Gaddafi? Or Qadhdhafi?

How do you spell the name of the former leader of Libya? In English, there is no one answer. His name might be spelled Qaddafi, Gaddafi, Khadafy, or Qadhdhafi. There are many different ways to convert the letters of the Arabic alphabet into the Latin alphabet, which is used to write English and other Western languages. As a result, the spelling of Arabic names in English-language publications varies. An Internet search might result in more than thirty possible spellings for the former leader's name. "Gaddafi" is the closest to how the name is pronounced in Libya, while "Qadhdhafi" is the most accurate reflection of how the name is written.

Revolt from the Inside

Throughout his decades as leader of Libya, Qaddafi used a variety of methods to hold on to power. He handpicked the leaders of his own tribe and other traditional allies. In this way, he was able to empower people who supported him. Qaddafi also kept his opponents weak. He sometimes used violence, having his opponents threatened, tortured, and murdered. He relied on elite troops to keep himself personally safe.

Many Libyans were unhappy with their lives and the tight control that Qaddafi held over them. So even while Qaddafi was trying to promote greater cooperation with the rest of the world, people in his own country were plotting to get rid of him.

Muammar Qaddafi (walking, second from left) attends an event with other North African leaders.

In February 2011, antigovernment rallies were held in Benghazi after a popular human rights lawyer was arrested. Libyan forces fired rubber bullets into the crowd and shot at the crowd with water cannons. Several protesters were injured.

Meanwhile, Libyans had witnessed uprisings against autocratic leaders in Tunisia and Egypt. This group of uprisings is known as the Arab Spring. Opposition leaders were inspired to overthrow the Qaddafi government in a similar way. As protests heated up, Qaddafi used force to put them down, and a civil war began.

In 2011, protests against authoritarian governments swept across the Arab world, including Libya.

The Battle of Sirte in 2011, which ended Qaddafi's rule, left many of the city's buildings in ruins.

International groups led air strikes against Qaddafi's forces as they threatened citizens. Fighting between the government troops and the opposition intensified as the United States and some European nations, especially France and Great Britain, provided assistance to those attempting to overthrow Qaddafi. By August 2011, Tripoli was under the control of the opposition force, called the National Transitional Council. Qaddafi and his family fled, seeking safety elsewhere in the country.

On October 20, 2011, during the Battle of Sirte, international forces helping the opposition bombed a convoy of some seventy-five vehicles that were fleeing Sirte. Qaddafi was in that convoy. He survived the bombing and fled on foot. The rebel troops soon captured him and then shot him.

Opposition leaders formed an acting government. But the country has seen continuing conflict since Qaddafi's death. His absence has left a huge hole, and as many as 1,700 armed groups are fighting to fill it. A second civil war began in 2014, and the government is extremely unstable.

Thousands of citizens have been killed. The nation's economy has suffered, too. Oil production has dropped because facilities have been blocked or damaged by the fighting. The country has lost some 90 percent of its oil income. Electricity frequently goes out. And business has stalled. Many residents have fled the country as refugees. Those who remain face great uncertainty.

Libyan children head for a rally celebrating the anniversary of the ouster of Muammar Qaddafi.

CHAPTER 5

A Government in Flux

DURING HIS FORTY-TWO-YEAR REIGN AS LEADER of Libya, Muammar Qaddafi kept tight control of the country. Libya was not free, but it was stable. Since the 2011 overthrow and murder of Qaddafi, Libya has been chaotic, and the government weak.

For the first few years after Qaddafi's death, sporadic violence broke out as militias and other factions vied for control. Elections were held in 2012, but conflict continued. No one was able to gain complete control.

Opposite: **Women show off their ink-stained fingers after voting in the 2012 elections. In Libya, people dip an index finger in ink when they cast their ballots to show that they have voted.**

Libya held a contest to write its national anthem in 1951, the year the nation became an independent kingdom. "Libya, Libya, Libya" won. Following the 1969 revolution that resulted in Qaddafi gaining control of the country, the anthem was replaced with "Allahu Akbar" ("God Is Great"), which is also the Muslim call to prayer. The old anthem was restored in 2011 after Qaddafi was killed.

English translation

O my country, O my country,
With my struggle and gladiatorial patience,
Drive off all enemies' plots and mishaps.
Be saved, be saved, be saved all the way.
We are your sacrifices.
Libya, Libya, Libya!

O my country, you're the heritage of my ancestors.
May Allah not bless any hand that tries to harm you.
Be saved, we are forever your soldiers.
No matter the death toll if you've been saved.
Take from us the most credential oaths.
We won't let you down, Libya.

We will never be enchained again.
We are free and have freed our homeland.
Libya, Libya, Libya!

Our grandfathers stripped a fine determination when
    the call for struggle was made.
They marched carrying the Qur'an in one hand, and
    their weapons by the other hand.
The universe is then full of faith and purity.
The world is then a place of goodness and godliness.
Eternity is for our grandfathers.
They have honored this homeland.
Libya, Libya, Libya!

Libya's Government of National Accord (GNA) was formed in late 2015. It is an interim government, meaning that it is only in place until a more permanent government can take over. The GNA is led by a prime minister and has seventeen ministers in charge of such fields as education, defense, finance, foreign affairs, and economy.

By 2014, there were two main rival governments operating in Libya. The first was the General National Congress (GNC), based in Tripoli. The second was the House of Representatives, based in the city of Tobruk. The House of Representatives is often called the Tobruk government. The United Nations tried to bring the two governments together in 2015 by creating the Government of National Accord (GNA).

Officials of the Government of National Accord take part in a meeting in 2016.

Khalifa Haftar

Perhaps the most influential leader in Libya is General Khalifa Haftar. He has had a lengthy military career and is known for having fought at one time or another on both sides of nearly every recent major conflict in Libya.

Born in eastern Libya in 1943, he served in the Libyan army under the command of Muammar Qaddafi, and took part in the revolution that put Qaddafi in power in 1969. For many years, he was a friend to Qaddafi, serving as a commander in the Libyan army. But in 1987, while he was a prisoner of war in Chad, he took part in a plot to overthrow Qaddafi. When it failed, he made his way to the United States and became a U.S. citizen. He lived in Virginia for nearly twenty years, though he did return to Libya briefly in 1996 to take part in another failed attempt to take down Qaddafi.

In 2011, Haftar went back to Libya to serve as a military leader of the rebel forces fighting Qaddafi. After Qaddafi's death, he did not get a role in the newly structured government, so he returned to the United States. But he was back in Libya by 2014 to lead the fight against Islamic militias in Benghazi, an effort he called "Operation Dignity."

In March 2015, Haftar became commander of the Libyan National Army, the military arm of the House of Representatives government based in Tobruk. Haftar and his military took control of Libya's major oil-producing region in September 2016. This move threatened the authority of the GNA, but his popular support in the area continued, and he remains one of the most powerful figures in the country.

Western leaders hoped the GNA would bring unity and provide solid leadership. But both rival governments must agree to the new plan. The GNC has joined with the GNA, but the Tobruk government has not.

Terrorism

The GNA faces opposition from several terrorist organizations operating in Libya. Some of them have been able to take over a small area. The most powerful of these is the Islamic State of Iraq and the Levant, often called ISIL, ISIS, or Daesh. For a time, it controlled the city of Sirte, and thousands of residents fled from there to escape the violence, leaving the city nearly empty. By late 2016, however, the militias working with the GNA had succeeded in taking control of Sirte away from ISIL.

The United States and other allied nations began launching air strikes against ISIL in August 2016. More than forty people were killed in one bombing, including a top terrorist

Tanks and forces loyal to the Government of National Accord roll through Sirte in 2016 during the effort to retake the city from ISIS terrorists.

A Look at the Capital

Libya's capital city of Tripoli was founded in the seventh century BCE by the Phoenicians. At the time, it was called Oea. Today, Tripoli is Libya's largest city, with 1,150,989 residents.

Tripoli is located on a rocky piece of land that juts out into the Mediterranean Sea, creating a bay. Because of this lovely location, Tripoli is sometimes called the Mermaid of the Mediterranean. The natural harbor has helped to make Tripoli the important seaport that it has been throughout its history. Oil and other petroleum products have been, and still are, sent out of the country on ships from Tripoli's ports; and in modern times, Tripoli is the center of Libya's economy.

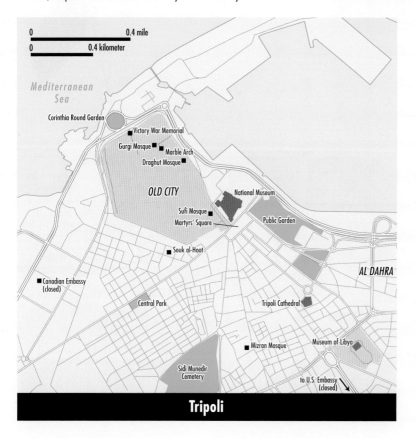

Tripoli's seaside promenade is a popular place for people to relax. Nearby is Martyrs' Square, a park full of palm trees. The city is home to Libya's National Museum and al-Fateh University, also known as the University of Tripoli. Tripoli's old quarter has a sixteenth-century Spanish fortress, ancient mosques, and a marble arch built by the Romans in the second century.

During the 2011 revolution, Tripoli was the site of several violent rallies, both for and against Qaddafi. Bombs rained down on the city. It suffered some destruction and continues to struggle amid all the instability in Libya.

National Flag

The Libyan Flag has three horizontal stripes, with red on top, a double width of black in the middle, and a green stripe on the bottom. A white star and a crescent are centered over the black stripe. The flag was chosen by Libya's transitional government following the overthrow of Qaddafi and his government.

The current flag marks a return to the flag that flew over the country from 1951 to 1969, when the country was the Kingdom of Libya. The designer, Omar Faiek Shennib, was a top government official under King Idris al-Sanusi. The red represents the blood sacrificed for Libya's freedom; the black reminds citizens of the dark days that Libyans lived through when their country was occupied by Italy, and the green represents the country's rich agriculture.

The transitional government chose this flag to replace the flag used during most of Qaddafi's reign. That flag was simply a field of vivid green, the traditional color of Islam.

leader. Some people believe that killing many of ISIL's members may convince others not to join the organization. But other people are concerned that sympathy or anger about the deaths may motivate some to join. Experts say that the people who join these groups often have no specific reason. Most members are young people who do not have jobs and do not see any hope in a terrible economy. They are angry and want revenge, but they don't know how to get it. They are looking for somewhere they can feel they belong.

In Libya, there is hope that the two rival governments will band together to combat ISIL. "By the grace of God, this will be the battle that unites Libyans," said one military commander.

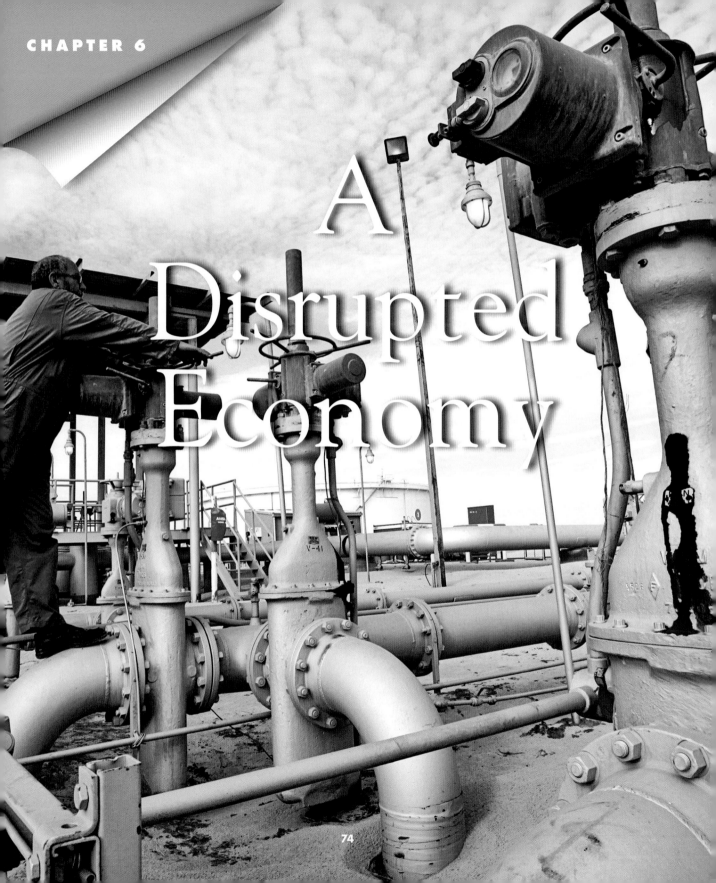

CHAPTER 6

A Disrupted Economy

WHEN MUAMMAR QADDAFI GAINED POWER IN Libya in 1969, it was one of the poorest nations in Africa. By the time he was killed in 2011, it had been one of Africa's wealthiest nations for decades. Most of the nation's income—95 percent of it—came from oil. But in recent years the country's wealth has declined as conflict has disrupted much of the nation. The nation's oil production has declined significantly.

Other businesses and industries are in equally bad shape. The unemployment rate is nearly 20 percent and is expected to remain high for some time. It's hard to keep things running when there is little stability. Electricity isn't always available. Transportation, too, is tricky; at times, it's not safe on the roads. And sometimes, the nation's gas stations have no gas to sell. Stores are often short of goods, and banks frequently have no cash.

Opposite: **A worker checks a valve at an oil field in eastern Libya. In the years of unrest following Libya's revolution, the nation's oil output dropped to just 20 percent of what it had once been.**

Money Facts

The basic unit of currency in Libya is the dinar. Each dinar is divided into 1,000 dirhams. In 2016, 1 dinar equaled US$0.71 while US$1.00 equaled 1.41 dinars.

Coins come in values of 50 and 100 dirhams and quarter and half dinars. There are also coins with values of 1, 5, 10, and 20 dirhams, but they're worth little and are rarely used. Paper money comes in values of quarter, half, 1, 5, 10, and 20 dinars. Each denomination has a different dominant color and depicts important Libyan sites or people. The 1 dinar note, for example, is pink and includes an image of anti-Qaddafi protesters. The blue 10-dinar note shows resistance fighter Omar al-Mukhtar. In 2016, competing currency was being printed by banks representing the two rival governments: the Government of National Accord based in Tripoli, and the House of Representatives based in Tobruk. The banknotes look similar, but some of the security features and serial numbers are different.

Oil is the main source of government income. Without it, there is little money available for schools, roads, and other public services. Corrupt politicians are a problem in the Libyan economy, too. Out of 175 countries ranked on how corrupt their public sector is, Libya ranked near the worst, at 170.

The Oil Industry

Libya holds more oil reserves than any other country in Africa, and it has one of the largest reserves in the world. Its oil is in high demand around the world because it contains less sulfur than oil from other places. This makes it cheaper to produce and cleaner to use. At one time, many Libyans worked in

What Libya Grows, Makes, and Mines

AGRICULTURE

Wheat (2016)	160,000 metric tons
Barley (2016)	90,000 metric tons
Chickens (2014)	34 million birds

MANUFACTURING (2015)

Steel	352,000 metric tons
Chemical products	$171,000,000 in exports
Machines	$18,500,000 in exports

MINING

Oil (2016)	330,000 barrels a day
Natural gas (2015)	15.5 million cubic meters

the oil industry and earned high wages. They bought modern appliances and goods. As more and more people purchased these items, other people got jobs making them. Shops sprang up to sell the goods, and the cycle continued. But this is no longer an accurate picture of Libya's economy.

Oil production is much lower than it was when Qaddafi was in power. At that time, the country produced an average of 1.4 million barrels of oil each day. With all the fighting since Qaddafi was overthrown, Libya's oil output has dropped to less than one-quarter of what it once was.

In addition to oil, Libya also has large quantities of natural gas. It has an estimated 46.4 trillion cubic feet (1.3 trillion cu m) in natural gas reserves, the fourth-largest supply in Africa.

A worker harvests barley on a farm near Tripoli.

Agriculture

Agriculture plays a small part in Libya's economy. Less than 2 percent of the land is considered arable, or suitable for growing crops. Most of the nation's farmland is along the Mediterranean coast. Cereals are the major crops and barley is the most common. Olives, almonds, and apricots are also grown. Because rainfall is low, irrigation is necessary. Most water for agriculture comes through the Great Man-Made River, which was disrupted after it was bombed in 2011.

In rural areas, many people raise livestock. These include sheep, goats, camels, and cattle. Chickens are also common.

Although Libya has a long stretch of Mediterranean coastline, it does not have a major fishing industry. The waters offshore don't have the right plankton to attract fish. Some of the fish that are caught include sardines, tuna, and mullet.

Industry

Construction is a growing business in Libya, as the country struggles to rebuild after the damage in the recent turmoil. The government is investing what resources it has in roads, airports, schools, hospitals, and railways. Libya's cement producers are having difficulty keeping up, though. Even though it is a large part of Libya's manufacturing, cement production is only about half of what it once was, due to aging facilities and war damage.

Libya also produces chemicals, iron, steel, and aluminum. There are food processing plants, as well as industries that produce textiles and leather goods. Salt and gypsum are also produced in Libya.

Resources

Oasis cultivation		Cem	Cement
Intensive cultivation		Fe	Iron
Shifting cultivation with livestock		⚒	Oil
Grazing		K	Potassium
Nonagricultural		Salt	Salt

CHAPTER 7

The People
of Libya

LIBYAN CITIES HAVE ALWAYS BEEN BUSY CENTERS of trade, with an international flair. For thousands of years, people have crossed the Mediterranean Sea by boat, linking Libya to many major European nations. In addition, Libya has long been a major stop for travelers between the Middle East and countries of North Africa farther to the west. Over the generations, some of the visitors to the cities along the coast have chosen to stay, adding to the ethnic diversity. Most Libyans make their homes in the narrow strip of land along the coast.

The communities in central Libya, where about 20 percent of Libya's residents live, are very different. In the past, these rural desert villages were ruled by chieftains, and little has changed over the centuries.

Opposite: **Women shop at a market in Tripoli.**

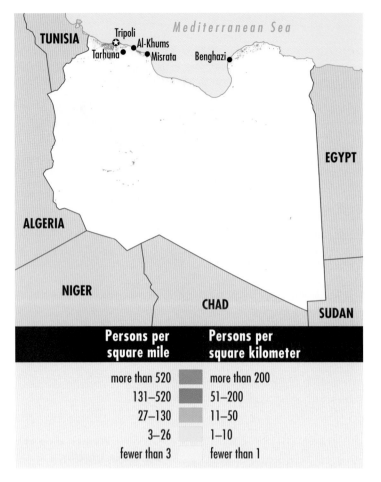

Mediterranean Sea

TUNISIA
Tripoli
Al-Khums
Tarhuna
Misrata
Benghazi

EGYPT

ALGERIA

NIGER

CHAD

SUDAN

Persons per square mile		Persons per square kilometer	
more than 520		more than 200	
131–520		51–200	
27–130		11–50	
3–26		1–10	
fewer than 3		fewer than 1	

A Snapshot of Libyans

Total population (2016 est.)	6,330,159
Percentage living in urban areas	79%
Percentage Berbers and Arabs	97%
Percentage other ethnic backgrounds	3%

Nomadic Ancestors

The ancestors of some Libyans were nomads. They moved from place to place, setting up camp wherever they could graze their animals and gather food and water. Nothing came easily in the desert, but people lived this way in Libya's Sahara for thousands of years. Today, only a small handful of Libyans still follow this ancient way of life.

Berbers once inhabited most of North Africa. Today, most Libyans have mixes of Berber and Arab ancestry. Berbers once lived as farmers in small groups along the coast. But as cities grew, Berbers were pushed out. Most moved to the Nafusa highlands near Tripoli, and lived a partially nomadic life in order to find food and water for their goats and sheep.

One group of Berbers is the Tuareg, who live in many countries in North Africa. Some Tuareg are known for their distinctive blue clothing. The Tuareg once carried goods across the Sahara on camel. Today, there are few truly nomadic Tuareg. Those that are nomadic live very different lives from their ancestors. Most travel using pickup trucks instead of camels, and they rarely carry regular goods for trade. Instead,

they are often forced to make a living by helping migrants cross the desert to the north, or by smuggling weapons.

The Bedouin are nomadic groups of Arabs who came to Libya in the eleventh century. Most now live in small farming communities near oases.

Libya is also home to a small number of groups that are neither Berber nor Arab. The Tebu, for example, are an ethnic group living in southern Libya, as well as in neighboring Niger and Chad. Their language is related to those spoken by groups farther to the south. The Tebu are traditionally herders and farmers, and some are nomadic. Under Muammar Qaddafi, the Tebu suffered severe discrimination, and during the revolution they sided with the forces who ousted him.

The Tebu people of southern Libya are among the few ethnic groups in the nation who are not Arab or Berber.

Population of Major Cities (2016 est.)

Tripoli	1,150,989
Benghazi	650,629
Misrata	386,120
Tarhuna	210,697
Al-Khums	201,943

Foreigners and Migration

Nearly half a million foreigners in Libya live in ramshackle old school buildings and camps. They had been living and working in Libya, but due to the civil war they no longer have any way of earning money or getting safely out of the country.

Another 250,000 or so entered Libya from other war-torn countries—Syria, Afghanistan, the Ivory Coast, Nigeria, Pakistan, and Gambia. They hoped simply to pass through Libya toward the coast and had no desire to live there.

Many migrants seeking to flee Africa and reach Europe go through Libya. In the past, it was more common for people to pass through Morocco, but today more people go through Libya. This is because without an effective government, Libya has little security to keep migrants out. It also has a long coastline from which people can depart across the Mediterranean. Getting to Libya can be expensive for migrants; many pay the equivalent of several hundred U.S. dollars just to ride atop trucks crossing the desert. They risk their lives where there is little water and temperatures reach dangerous highs. Even if the migrants make it to the coast, they still have difficulty get-

A boat overloaded with migrants headed for Italy begins to capsize off the Libyan coast. Thousands of migrants have died trying to cross the Mediterranean.

ting aboard a smuggler's boat. While waiting for their chance, most live desperate lives in Libya's coastal cities. They have no way to earn a living and are often the victims of crime.

For those who do get on boats, the journey is dangerous. The Mediterranean crossing is rough and can be especially risky on rickety vessels overloaded with passengers. Thousands have died. Thousands more have been rescued.

Each year tens of thousands of migrants who pass through Libya make it to Europe. Most land in Italy. Italy and other European nations have struggled to provide medical care, food, shelter, and jobs to the refugees.

Language

Arabic is the main language in Libya, and has been since the Islamic invasion in the seventh century. On the street, Libyans speak a distinctive form of Arabic, with local terms and accents. But in schools, business, and government, Libyans speak Modern Standard Arabic.

In the western mountains and the desert oases, some people speak the Berber language, called Tamazight. The Tuareg people also speak Tamazight.

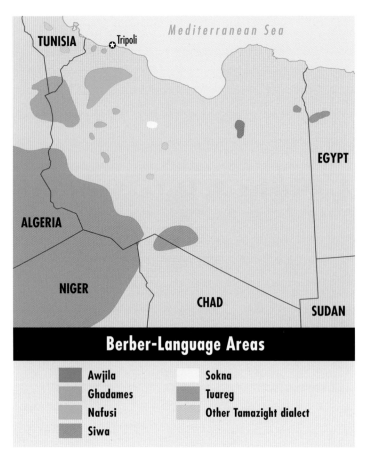

Berber-Language Areas

Awjila
Ghadames
Nafusi
Siwa
Sokna
Tuareg
Other Tamazight dialect

Common Arabic Words and Phrases

aiwa/naam	yes
la	no
min fadlek	please
shukran	thank you
insha' allah	God willing
assalamu alakum	hello
bisalama	good-bye
sabaah al-khair	good morning
masa' al-khair	good evening
ismah-lee	excuse me
asif	I am sorry
Bikam?	How much?
Kam kilometric...?	How far to...?
Keef halek?	How are you?

Arabic is written from right to left, the opposite of how English is written.

The People of Libya   **87**

CHAPTER 8

Mostly Muslim

NEARLY EVERYONE IN LIBYA—97 PERCENT OF THE
population—is Muslim, or followers of Islam. It is the country's national religion.

Islam has its roots in the visions that the Prophet
Muhammad had, beginning in the year 610. He was forty
years old at the time, living in the city of Mecca in what
is now Saudi Arabia. Muslims believe that in these visions,
Muhammad received messages from God, called *Allah* in

Opposite: **A Tuareg man
holds prayer beads.**

A mosque, or Muslim place of worship, in northeastern Libya. Mosques serve as places to pray, but they also usually provide education and social services.

Arabic, delivered by the angel Gabriel. Gabriel is said to have told Muhammad about the "Word of God," and explained how people should live, what they should believe, and how they should worship.

The word *Islam*, in Arabic, means "submission to the will of God," and *Muslim* means "one who submits." Muhammad submitted to his duty and shared these messages, but few people listened to him at first. Powerful people of Mecca despised his teaching that God was the one great power. They

The Qur'an

Muhammad eventually wrote down the messages he received in his visions, and they were compiled into Islam's holy book, the Qur'an. Qur'an is an Arabic word meaning "recitation." Muslims believe the Qur'an records the words of God. Many Muslims make a practice of reading a part of the Qur'an every day. It is divided into thirty equal parts, each taking a bit less than one-half hour to read. There are a total of 114 chapters.

were upset when Muhammad ordered people to share their wealth with the poor. Muhammad's life was threatened over these teachings, so in 622 he left Mecca. He began his journey north to Medina, also in today's Saudi Arabia.

This journey, known as the *hijrah*, gave Muhammad an opportunity to preach to people who were open to his teachings. He attracted many followers in Medina. In 630, Muhammad led them on his return to Mecca, and it became Islam's holy city.

Muhammad died in 632 but Islam continued to spread. As traders sailed the sea and crossed the desert, they brought their faith with them, sharing it as they went. Arab soldiers who were followers of Islam conquered other countries. Residents of the conquered lands became Muslims, too, and in less than one century, Muslim lands stretched from Spain in the west to Afghanistan in the east.

In Libya, people had long-held religious beliefs before the introduction of Islam. When the Carthaginians ruled the land, their strong faith influenced Libyan religion. They

A Coptic Christian lights a candle at a mass in Misrata. The Coptic Orthodox Church is the largest Christian sect in Libya.

Religion in Libya

Sunni Muslims 97%

Other Muslims,
Christians, Buddhists 3%

believed in many gods with great powers. After Egyptians introduced Christianity to the region, it became a popular faith in the eastern part of Libya. Libya also had a large Jewish population for centuries.

Beliefs of Islam

Allah is the same God that Christians and Jews worship. Many of the teachings and stories in the Qur'an are similar to those found in the Old Testament of the Bible, and prophets of Judaism and Christianity are respected in Islam. Muslims believe that Jesus Christ was a great teacher and prophet, but they do not believe that he was the son of God, as Christians do. Muslims also believe in final judgment of heaven or hell for people after their death.

Islam is divided into two main groups: Sunnis and Shi'is. Shi'is believe that the leader of Islam should be a direct descendant of Muhammad. Sunnis accept others in that role. Today almost all Muslims in Libya are Sunnis.

Libya is also home to a community of Ibadis, members of a third branch of Islam. Ibadism is the dominant form of Islam in the Middle Eastern country of Oman but is rare elsewhere. The Ibadis claim that their group is older than the other branches of Islam. In Libya, Ibadis are primarily found in the Nafusa highlands among people who speak Tamazight.

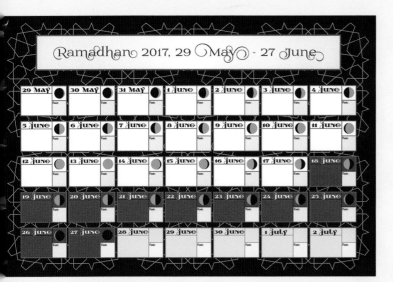

The Islamic Calendar

The Islamic calendar is lunar, meaning that it is determined by the phases of the moon. A month is the period between two new moons. It differs from the calendar commonly used throughout the world, the Gregorian calendar, which is based on the solar year. Muslims follow both calendars, with the Islamic calendar determining their holy days. While the solar calendar has 365 days in a year, the Islamic calendar year has just 354 days. This means that the dates of Muslim holidays fall eleven days earlier in the Gregorian calendar each year.

The first month of the Islamic calendar year is Muharram, and the first day is Ras al-Sanah, the Muslim New Year. This day commemorates the beginning of Islamic history, the day in 622 when Muhammad began the hijrah from Mecca to Medina.

Religious Holidays

Religious holidays of Islam are based on the Muslim lunar calendar and fall on different dates and in different months, according to the Gregorian calendar used by many nations.

Ras al-Sanah (Muslim New Year)
Eid al-Fitr (End of Ramadan)
Eid al-Adha (Feast of the Sacrifice)

The ritual of praying on Eid al-Fitr, the holiday marking the end of Ramadan, includes applying perfume. Here, a boy dabs men's hands with perfume before a prayer session.

In addition, Libya has a population of Sufi Muslims, who have played a significant role in the nation's history. Libyan hero Omar al-Mukhtar, for example, was a Sufi. Sufism is a more mystical and emotional form of Islam. In the chaos since

the 2011 revolution, some extreme fundamentalist groups have attacked Sufi shrines because they do not consider Sufism the correct type of Islam.

Sufi Muslims chant and beat drums during a procession celebrating Muhammad's birthday.

Rules for Muslim Life

Islam strongly influences the lives of most Libyans. Like Muslims everywhere, they follow certain practices known as the Five Pillars of Islam.

One of the Five Pillars states that Muslims should pray five times daily. The mosque, the Muslim house of worship, is central to each city or village. Traditionally, Muslims were called to prayer by a *muezzin*, a man who stood in the minaret, a tower near the entrance of the mosque. Now, typically, the call to prayer is prerecorded and broadcast through speakers.

Another of the pillars encourages Muslims to make a religious journey, or pilgrimage, to the holy city of Mecca. This pilgrimage, known as the *hajj*, occurs during the twelfth month of the Islamic calendar. Each year, about two million people take part, making it the largest annual gathering of people in the world. In Mecca, pilgrims visit Islam's holiest shrine, a cube-shaped building called the Kaaba. During a ritual called *tawaf*, pilgrims walk seven times counterclockwise around the Kaaba.

Women pray in Martyrs' Square in Tripoli. Muslims always pray facing in the direction of Mecca, Saudi Arabia, Islam's holiest city.

The Five Pillars of Islam

Just as the pillars of a building give it strength and structure, the Five Pillars of Islam give structure to the lives of Muslims.

The first pillar of Islam is *shahada*, or witnessing. Muslims must make a public statement of faith. They say a verse in Arabic that translates to "I bear witness that there is no god but God, and Muhammad is the messenger of God." They must declare this with genuine belief.

Salat, or prayer, is the second pillar. Muslims are obliged to pray five times each day, at dawn, at noon, in midafternoon, at sunset, and in the evening.

The third pillar is *zakat*, or charity. Muslims are obliged to share their money with those in need, including the poor, new converts to Islam, Muslim prisoners of war, and foreigners seeking help.

Sawm, or fasting, is the fourth pillar of Islam. Muslims do not eat, drink, or smoke during daylight hours of Ramadan, the ninth month of the Muslim calendar. To Muslims, it is an act of worship that gives them a sense of devotion, moderation, discipline, maturity, and unity.

The fifth pillar is *hajj* (above). This is the requirement that every Muslim make a pilgrimage, or visit, to Mecca at least once in his or her lifetime, if at all possible.

In addition to the Five Pillars of Islam, there are other rules. Muslims are not supposed to drink liquor or gamble. They may not eat pork. They may lend money but must not charge interest. They must be respectful, honest, and generous with others.

Religious Holidays

Ramadan, the ninth month of the Islamic calendar, is a holy month for Muslims. They believe that this is when Muhammad received the first of many revelations from God. Muslims fast for the entire month, eating and drinking only before sunrise and after sundown. Fasting, they believe, improves spiritual life by cleansing the body and increasing compassion for poor people. The meal that breaks the fast each evening is called *iftar*.

Muslims celebrate the end of Ramadan with a three-day festival called Eid al-Fitr. They exchange gifts, buy new

Volunteers in Benghazi prepare food that will be distributed for the iftar meal. During Ramadan, people often gather for large communal meals.

clothes, donate to charity, and enjoy delicious foods with family and friends.

Muhammad's birthday, Mawlid al-Nabawi, is an important religious and legal holiday. Muslims study the Prophet's words and life, and finish off the day with firecrackers, music, dance, and shared meals. Another holy day, Eid al-Adha, the Feast of the Sacrifice, recalls Abraham's willingness to sacrifice his son for God. The festival marks the end of the annual pilgrimage to Mecca.

Alaa Murabit

Alaa Murabit is working to ensure that women have a voice in Libya's peace process, and she believes that the Muslim faith leads the way. Murabit was born in 1989 in Canada, but is of Libyan heritage and moved to Zawiya, Libya, with her family when she was fifteen. There she enrolled in medical school, becoming a doctor at age twenty-four. She was frustrated to see the prejudice and violence against women often excused with religion.

"Young girls need to know that they can fight fire with fire and say 'No, my religion is not why you are doing this,'" Murabit has said. She got in trouble fighting for women's rights and had to hide out for several months in order to avoid arrest. Following the 2011 revolution, she founded the Voice of Libyan Women (VLW) when she was just twenty-one.

Murabit hopes to empower women by educating them on the teachings of their faith, using verses from the Qur'an and other Muslim wisdom. This way, they will be better able to participate in government and speak out for their rights.

Murabit has received many awards for her work. In 2016, she became the youngest person appointed to the United Nations Sustainable Development Goals Advocates. She's also done a TED Talk about women's rights in Islam. In it she asks: "Why if we are equal in the eyes of God are we not equal in the eyes of men?"

CHAPTER 9

The Arts Coming Alive

THE ARTS IN LIBYA, LIKE NEARLY EVERYTHING ELSE there, are in transition. For decades under Qaddafi's rule, musicians, writers, and artists were cautious about their creations. If they offended the dictator or his family there could be trouble. Some got a threatening visit from one of Qaddafi's officers. Artists were also imprisoned and killed.

Opposite: **Metalwork is a traditional Libyan craft. The Copper Souk in Tripoli offers many crescents for the tops of minarets in mosques.**

Once Qaddafi had been ousted, the arts began to flourish in Libya. With their new freedoms, artists had plenty of emotional material to inspire them and the opportunity to express themselves without fear. Literature was published; films were made. But this freedom didn't last long. Strict Islamist radicals rose to power in various parts of the country and stifled artists once again. Libyan artists today must still be careful in certain areas of the country. Some have left Libya in search of freedom of expression elsewhere.

A man walks by street art in Tripoli.

Poetry and Literature

Poetry is an important art form in Libya. Many Libyans memorize poems and recite them for others. Most of these poems are old, and many encourage the fight for freedom and independence. Qaddafi made sure that published works of literature and poetry did not threaten his government.

In 2012, one year after the end of the Qaddafi reign, a few poets quickly arranged the first ever Tripoli International Poetry Festival. The three-day event was a success, with poets coming from countries around the world. Khaled Mattawa from Libya, the festival's organizer, shared his poems. With the festival's success, plans were made to expand it in the future, adding art and music workshops, video installations, and guest

The Tripoli International Poetry Festival also includes music and other folk art performances.

speakers. But none of this has come to pass because of the ongoing violence and political upheaval. To ensure his own safety, Mattawa moved to the United States.

Art

Traditional Libyan arts such as leatherwork, metal engraving, weaving, jewelry making, pottery, and embroidery are crafts that have been handed down through generations. Some

Some Libyans learn traditional crafts from their parents or on the job. Others can learn crafts at institutions like the Islamic Arts and Crafts School in Tripoli.

craftspeople decorate everyday items such as blankets, dishes, and belts with traditional designs.

The religion of the craftspeople is reflected in their art. Following Muslim tradition, most Libyan artists do not depict humans or living creatures in their work. They believe that making an image of a life-form is trespassing on God's role as the creator. Instead, Islamic arts feature elaborate geometric patterns. Such designs, called arabesque, enliven many mosques and buildings.

Libya's visual arts are progressing more rapidly than literature and poetry. Even during the later years of Qaddafi's rule, modern art and fashion were becoming popular, especially in major cities such as Tripoli and Benghazi. Though the country has few art museums, there are private galleries where Libyan artists show their work.

The Karamanli Mosque in Tripoli is renowned for the intricate designs on its tiles.

In the oasis town of Ghadames, the whitewashed walls of houses are often painted with traditional red designs.

International galleries also give Libyan artists a space to display their art on occasion. The Arab British Center in London, for example, showcased the work of several Libyan artists in 2015. Their pieces reflected on the history of Libya's two major cities, Tripoli and Benghazi, and the changes seen

The National Museum

Libya's National Museum, located in Tripoli, has one of the finest collections of classical art in the Mediterranean region. Artifacts from when Romans and Greeks ruled Libya are among the treasures on display there. The museum was built with help from UNESCO, and many pieces were collected from Libya's World Heritage Sites at Leptis Magna and Sabratha. Its forty-seven galleries offer a comprehensive look at Libyan history, from ancient times through the present day.

in recent times. Artists showed through paintings and sculpture that war is a major part of life in Libya, and how they can break free, at least for a moment, through beauty. They represented the hope that peace and unity will return to Libya.

Music

Music is a part of almost all religious and social ceremonies and festivities in Libya. Rhythm is an important element; people clap their hands while others play drums and tambourines. Musical instruments that have been used in Libya for

In Libya, people of different ethnic groups often produce different types of jewelry. The jewelry of the Tuareg people uses a lot of silver.

The oud does not have a standard number of strings. The most common number is eleven, but it can have up to thirteen.

centuries include the *oud*, a stringed instrument similar to a lute; the *darbuka*, a goblet-shaped drum; and the *al-nay*, a kind of bamboo pipe.

Some traditional folk songs handed down by nomadic groups speak lovingly of desert sands or tell of journeys across the Sahara. Others tell of great triumphs in history or of difficult struggles faced long ago.

A well-known singer named Ayman al-Aatar performs more modern tunes in addition to traditional ones. Born in Tripoli in 1982, he was the winner of the 2004 Arab version of *American Idol*. Al-Aatar is still popular, performing music that blends Western and Libyan influences.

During his long reign, Qaddafi controlled the nation's music, making sure there was nothing that could stir up opposition to him. American music was outlawed, and most songs played on the radio were by Qaddafi's favorite musicians.

That all began to change in 2011 with the start of the revolution. Protest music helped inspire people. "We Will Not Surrender" became a popular song just as the revolt was beginning. It used the words of the Libyan war hero Omar al-Mukhtar. Rami El-Kaleh, who recorded the song, was assassinated by Qaddafi's fighters within days of recording it.

Asma Salim's songs also motivated Libyans during the revolution. Though Salim was born in Libya, she moved with

Ayman al-Aatar signs autographs for fans.

Musicians often joined protesters in the uprising against Qaddafi's regime.

her family to Tunisia to escape the difficulties of life under Qaddafi. Still, she often sang about her hopes for freedom in her home country. Once Qaddafi was gone, she returned to Libya, and her music is heard throughout North Africa.

Rap has also gained popularity in Libya. Ibn Thabit is the stage name of a Libyan rapper, about whom not much is known. His name comes from the history of Islam: Zayd ibn Thabit was the scribe for Muhammad, the person who wrote

"The Issue"

One of Ibn Thabit's songs was particularly popular among those taking part in the uprising against Muammar Qaddafi in 2011. Called "The Issue," its lyrics include these lines:

Muammar, you have never served the people.
Muammar, you'd better give up.
Confess. You cannot escape.
Our revenge will catch you.
As a train roars through a wall,
we will drown you.

down his words. The young singer took this name because he felt that he was writing words for his fellow Libyans, expressing their views through his songs. He wrote protest songs during the revolution and shared his music through social media.

Sports

Many Libyans take part in sports. Soccer is the country's most popular sport. Throughout Libya, children play soccer on organized teams and on the streets. Adults play on local teams, and their games often have big audiences. The highest

A young Libyan shows off his skill at a street soccer event in Benghazi.

level of Libyan soccer is the Libyan Premier League, founded in 1963. It has sixteen teams.

The Premier League is dominated by two teams based in Tripoli, Al Ittihad and Al Ahli. They play in a stadium that seats eighty-eight thousand people, and many more people watch the games on television.

Professional soccer games were not played for a couple of years following the 2011 revolution. The games returned for the 2013–2014 season but were marked by violence when snipers shot the coach and a key player on Tripoli's Al Ahli team. Neither were seriously injured, but many more players received death threats. The attacks were linked to the political divisions that separate the country, and were believed to come from terrorist organizations. Because of this danger, most soccer players in Libya tend to keep a low profile, and as a result don't earn the celebrity status that top athletes get in some countries.

Libyans also enjoy other sports. Basketball has long been popular. Along the coast, some people make time for swimming, diving, and even waterskiing. Large cities have golf courses, bowling alleys, and tennis courts. In the years since Qaddafi was ousted, skateboarding has become popular among young people.

Young Libyans play basketball at a park in Tripoli. The sport has been growing in popularity in recent years.

CHAPTER 10

Life Goes On

LIFE IN LIBYA HAS BEEN UNCERTAIN IN RECENT years. In 2016, experts estimated that nearly 2.5 million people needed such basic services as clean water, health care, and education. The electricity often doesn't work, and stores don't have a lot to offer. One in five adults is out of work. Nearly half a million people have been forced out of their homes.

Still, in most places in Libya, life goes on. People continue to enjoy spending time with family and friends and sharing meals. Many Libyans try to tune out the background threat of violence. They believe that is the best choice they can make.

Opposite: **A Libyan father relaxes with his daughter. The average Libyan family has two children.**

Couscous is a staple food throughout North Africa.

Food

Libyans eat a wide variety of foods. They usually buy their ingredients at outdoor markets called *souks*. Vendors set up tables that overflow with colorful fruits and vegetables. Shoppers bargain with the vendors to get the best price.

Many Libyan dishes are stews that are sometimes spicy. Libya's national dish is couscous, which is a type of pasta made from crushed wheat, and rolled into tiny bits like rice. It's the base of the meal and served with a variety of sauces and vegetables. Cooks will mix in hot peppers, tomatoes, and vegetables. It is prepared in a pot that everyone eats from. Another common menu item is *kasrah*, a type of flatbread. People tear off a piece and use it to scoop dip from a shared bowl.

Meat is eaten only occasionally. The most common meat consumed in Libya is lamb. People also eat chicken, beef, and camel. Libyans who live near the coast eat some seafood. Figs, apricots, and oranges are popular fruits. Libyans often finish a meal with a piece of fruit and some green tea.

Vendors set up piles of oranges at a market in Tripoli. January is orange harvest season in Libya.

Shakshuka

Shakshuka is a traditional Libyan dish that is also popular in many nations around the Mediterranean. It is a good example of local fare: simple, delicious, and spicy. It is also flexible—ingredients can easily be left out, depending upon what is available. The tasty sauce can be scooped up with flatbread. Have an adult help you with this recipe.

Ingredients

1 jalapeño pepper

1 red pepper

1 small onion

6 cloves garlic

¼ cup olive oil

2 teaspoons paprika

1 teaspoon cumin

2 14-ounce cans diced tomatoes

1 teaspoon salt

½ cup water

8 eggs

1 tablespoon chopped parsley

Directions

Carefully remove the seeds and stems from the jalapeño pepper, and then chop it finely. Chop the red pepper, onion, and garlic.

Heat the oil in a medium skillet, and add the peppers and onion. Cook them over high heat until they are soft, stirring occasionally. Add the garlic, paprika, and cumin. Continue cooking until the garlic is soft. Add the tomatoes, salt, and a half cup of water. Cook over medium heat for about 20 minutes, until slightly thickened.

Crack the eggs and carefully slide them into the sauce mix. Try to keep the yolks intact, and cover the surface of the sauce with eggs evenly. Cover the skillet and cook for about 5 minutes over low heat until the eggs are set. Use a spoon to scoop some of the sauce mixture over the eggs, trying not to disturb them. Cook a minute or two longer, until the eggs are done. Sprinkle parsley over the top. Enjoy!

Many Libyans enjoy Western-style fast foods such as hamburgers and fried chicken. Before the fall of Qaddafi, Western restaurant chains were not allowed in the country, so enterprising Libyans got creative. They started fast-food shops such as Uncle Kentaki, selling—what else?—crispy fried chicken. These fast-food places continue to thrive in Libya.

A man grills chicken at a take-out restaurant in Tripoli.

Clothing

According to the Qur'an, men and women should dress modestly. This idea has been interpreted in many different ways. Some Muslim women wear veils in public to cover their hair or faces. Others also wear long, loose robes that cloak their clothing. Some women in Libya follow this style of dress through

A Tuareg girl dresses in traditional clothing for a festival.

Fashion of Fadwa Baruni

Libyan clothing designer Fadwa Baruni trained to be a petroleum engineer, but her interests quickly turned to fashion. In 2008 she launched her clothing line, Baruni Couture. Now based in the United Arab Emirates, Baruni is a popular clothing designer for women who want to be fashionable but also follow the rules of their Muslim faith.

Baruni's gowns are sold throughout the world, but they are especially popular in the Middle East. She incorporates her Libyan heritage into her clothing by frequently using the warm colors of the Mediterranean coast.

their own choice, while in areas controlled by fundamentalist Islamists, they are required to cover themselves from head to toe when they are outside. At home, however, they remove their veils and coverings in the parts of their homes where they will be seen only by women and close male relatives.

Traditionally, the clothing worn by Libyan men varied by region and ethnic background. In desert regions, men wore long robes that protected them from the heat of the sun. Along the coast, embroidered vests were common. Today, most Libyan men have adopted Western styles such as suits, T-shirts, and jeans. Others wear long, loose tunics and slacks with sandals.

Becoming a Family

Weddings in Libya are rich in tradition. Some of these traditions are fading, however. In the past, most marriages were arranged—parents selected partners for their children. But in recent decades, it has become common for young Libyans to choose their spouses themselves, though family approval is still important.

Another fading tradition is the custom of men providing homes and lavish furnishings and gold for their brides. Couples are no longer getting married in their teens as frequently as Libyans once did. With so many men out of work, they do not have much money with which to marry or start

A woman photographs a bride at her wedding celebration. Some Libyan brides choose Western-style dresses.

Henna Poisoning

Henna tattoos are popular among women in Libya. Henna is the powdered leaf of a shrub. The powder is made into a paste and then painted on women's hands, arms, and feet, usually in detailed designs. Afterward, it is left to dry, often for several hours, as the reddish-brown color is absorbed into the skin. When the paste is washed off, the design can remain for weeks or months.

Henna tattoos are often incorporated into marriage ceremonies in Libya, but women also get them at other times as well. They enjoy the beautiful designs and appreciate their symbolism. Henna tattoos are a centuries-old tradition that have been used safely by millions of women in Libya and elsewhere.

However, getting a henna tattoo has become more dangerous for Libyan women since 2011, when strict controls were removed after Qaddafi's death. Some manufacturers have started to add a dangerous chemical compound, para-phenylenediamine, to the paste.

It makes the henna darker, but it is toxic and has been banned in many countries, though not Libya. Since 2011, more than one hundred Libyan women have died after getting a henna tattoo.

a family. Women are expected to work outside the home, so many want to postpone marriage to get an education and improve their chance for a career. Also, there is a shortage of affordable housing for young couples. For all these reasons, many are putting off marriage to a later time.

Still, couples who do get married sometimes enjoy traditional Libyan weddings. These can last a full week and are often quite expensive. It is considered an honor for young Libyans to have children as soon as possible after they are married.

A teenager studies at a Libyan school. Libyans are required to attend school until age fifteen.

Children

The lives of children, like those of their families, have been disrupted by Libya's political turmoil. Nearly six hundred schools across the country were closed in 2016 due to damage from fighting, keeping some 279,000 children out of school. Even schools that were open felt the effects of the civil war. The start of the 2016–2017 school year was delayed for several months in parts of Libya because of a lack of schoolbooks. Officials from the rival governments were not cooperating, and though the books had been shipped to the eastern Tobruk government, they were not shared with those living in the west.

UNICEF is trying to help Libyan kids get back to a normal childhood. Starting in 2016, the organization began distributing recreational and educational kits to tens of thousands of Libyan children. The recreational boxes contain such things as balls, paints, building blocks, and puzzles, as well as games to teach basic math and reading. The educational kits, called School-in-a-Box, contain wooden clocks and cubes, workbooks, solar radios, posters, pencils, and scissors.

UNICEF's School-in-a-Box contains supplies for forty students and a teacher. The kit includes paint that can be used to turn the box into a blackboard. This allows teachers to set up schools anywhere.

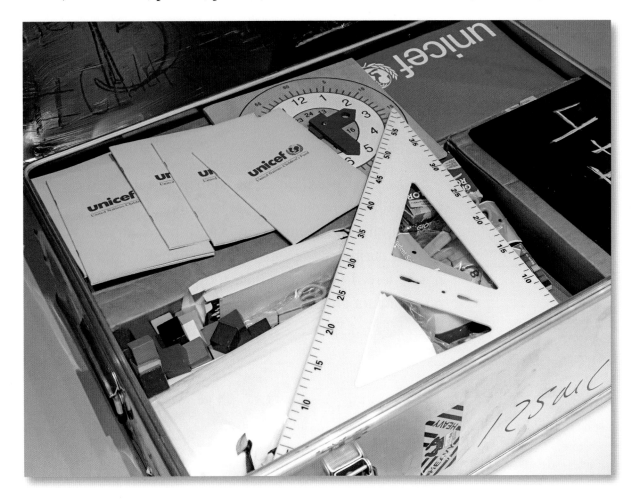

Foosball is a popular game in Libya. Tables are set up outdoors in many cities.

"The longer a child's education is disrupted, the higher the likelihood that it will never be complete," said a UNICEF representative. "Children in Libya have already suffered enough during the recent violence and conflict. They must not be forced to sacrifice their future as well. The conflict is no excuse for children not to be learning."

Childhood Games

Libyan children love to play outside, and many of their favorite games are much like games played by children living in the West. *Wabees* is a lot like hide-and-seek, while *negayza* is similar to hopscotch. *Seyad al sakkara* is a form of dodgeball.

Hope for the Future

In 2016, Libya began a project aimed at increasing social tolerance. The Education Ministry is working to increase the acceptance students show to others in order to diminish the violence that is so damaging to Libya. They want to establish an atmosphere of peace and tolerance in schools.

Students attend workshops and seminars promoting peaceful coexistence. They read books and other publications showing how people can get along. They learn about how to accept other people with religious, ethnic, and political differences.

By promoting peace among Libya's young people, educators hope that peace will spread throughout the rest of the population. Young people, they believe, hold the key to a more positive future for Libya.

Boys walk by the National Museum in Tripoli, which was once a fortress.

Timeline

LIBYAN HISTORY

Sidi Muhammad ibn-Ali al-Sanusi establishes the Sanusi Brotherhood.	1837
Italy gains control of Libya.	1912
The Italians execute resistance Leader Omar al-Mukhtar.	1931
Libya is freed from Italian rule.	1943
Libya becomes an independent nation.	1951
Vast oil fields are discovered in Libya.	1959
Army officers seize control of Libya; Muammar Qaddafi becomes the country's new leader.	1969
Work begins on the Great Man-Made River.	1984
Pan Am flight 103 blows up over Lockerbie, Scotland; Libyan terrorists are believed to be responsible.	1988
Two Libyans are charged with bombing Pan Am flight 103; Qaddafi refuses to turn them over for trial.	1991
The United Nations bans air travel to and from Libya.	1992
Libya turns over suspects in the Pan Am flight 103 bombing for trial.	1999
There are large protests against Qaddafi; Qaddafi is overthrown and killed.	2011
Hundreds of groups fight for control of Libya.	2012
The Government of National Accord is formed, based in Tripoli.	2015

WORLD HISTORY

1865	The American Civil War ends.
1879	The first practical lightbulb is invented.
1914	World War I begins.
1917	The Bolshevik Revolution brings communism to Russia.
1929	A worldwide economic depression begins.
1939	World War II begins.
1945	World War II ends.
1969	Humans land on the Moon.
1975	The Vietnam War ends.
1989	The Berlin Wall is torn down as communism crumbles in Eastern Europe.
1991	The Soviet Union breaks into separate states.
2001	Terrorists attack the World Trade Center in New York City and the Pentagon near Washington, D.C.
2004	A tsunami in the Indian Ocean destroys coastlines in Africa, India, and Southeast Asia.
2008	The United States elects its first African American president.
2016	Donald Trump is elected U.S. president.

Fast Facts

Official name: Libya

Capital: Tripoli

Official language: Arabic

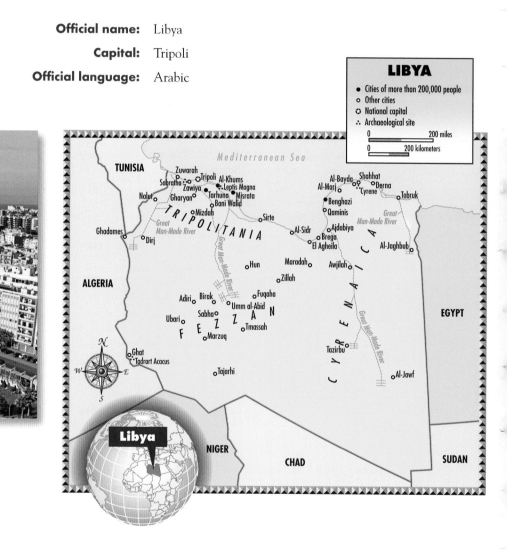

Benghazi

National flag

Nafusa Mountains

Official religion:	Islam
Year of founding:	1951, Kingdom of Libya
National anthem:	"Libya, Libya, Libya"
Type of government:	Interim government
Area:	679,362 square miles (1,759,540 sq km)
Greatest distance north to south:	930 miles (1,500 km)
Greatest distance east to west:	1,050 miles (1,700 km)
Coordinates of geographic center:	25°N, 17°E
Land and water borders:	Mediterranean Sea to the north, Egypt to the east, Sudan to the southeast, Chad and Niger to the south, Algeria and Tunisia to the west
Highest elevation:	Bikku Bitti, 7,438 feet (2,267 m) above sea level
Lowest elevation:	Sabkhat Ghuzayyil, 154 feet (47 m) below sea level
Average annual precipitation:	About 15 inches (38 cm) in Tripoli; less than 1 inch (2.5 cm) in the Sahara
Average high temperature:	In Tripoli, 64°F (17.5°C) in January, 96°F (36°C) in July; in Sabha, 65°F (18°C) in January, 102°F (39°C) in July
Average low temperature:	In Tripoli, 45°F (7°C) in January, 70°F (21°C) in July; in Sabha, 43°F (6°C) in January, 76°F (25°C) in July

Leptis Magna

National population (2016 est.): 6,330,159

Population of major cities (2016 est.):

Tripoli	1,150,989
Benghazi	650,629
Misrata	386,120
Tarhuna	210,697
Al-Khums	201,943

Landmarks:
- ▶ *Cyrene,* near Benghazi
- ▶ *Ghadames,* in the west
- ▶ *Leptis Magna,* near Tripoli
- ▶ *Marble Arch,* Tripoli
- ▶ *Tadrart Acacus,* near Ghat

Economy: Libya's economy has been in turmoil since the overthrow of Qaddafi in 2011. The oil industry traditionally dominates the Libyan economy. However, armed conflict between rival forces for control of oil terminals has caused a massive decline in output. The nation also produces natural gas and gypsum. Top manufacturing industries include oil production, iron and steel, cement, food processing, and textiles. The main crops grown in Libya are barley, wheat, and olives. Livestock raised in Libya includes chickens, sheep, and goats. Massive power outages, problems with transportation, and continued fighting have caused a drop in productivity and output throughout all areas of the economy.

Currency

Currency: The dinar. In 2016, 1 dinar equaled US$0.71, while US$1.00 equaled 1.41 dinars.

Weights and measures: The metric system plus some Arab weights and measures

Literacy rate: 91%

Student

Omar al-Mukhtar

Common Arabic words and phrases:

aiwa/naam	yes
la	no
min fadlek	please
shukran	thank you
assalamu alakum	hello
bisalama	good-bye
sabaah al-khair	good morning
masa' al-khair	good evening
ismah-lee	excuse me
asif	I am sorry

Prominent Libyans:

Ayman al-Aatar *Singer*	(1982–)
Omar al-Mukhtar *Resistance leader*	(1862–1931)
Alaa Murabit *Peace Activist*	(1989–)
Muammar Qaddafi *Political leader*	(1942–2011)
Idris al-Sanusi *King*	(1890–1983)

To Find Out More

Books

- ▶ Hasday, Judy. *Libya*. Broomhall, PA: Mason Crest Publishers, 2014.

- ▶ Hunter, Nick. *Libya*. Portsmouth, NH: Heinemann, 2012.

- ▶ O'Neal, Claire. *We Visit Libya*. Newark, DE: Mitchell Lane Publishers, 2013.

Music

- ▶ *Arabic Groove*. New York: Putumayo World Music, 2001.

- ▶ *Rough Guide to the Best Arabic Music You've Never Heard*. London: World Music Network, 2015.

▶ Visit this Scholastic website for more information on Libya:
www.factsfornow.scholastic.com
Enter the keyword **Libya**

Index

Page numbers in *italics* indicate illustrations.

central pivot irrigation, 25, *25*
Chad, 60, 70
children, *18*, *30*, 65, *94*, *114*, 123,
    124–126, *126*, 127
Christianity, 92
cities. *See also* Benghazi; towns;
    Tripoli; villages.
    Al-Khums, 19, *19*, 83
    Derna, 24
    Germa, *49*
    Leptis Magna, 46, *47*, 48, 106
    Misrata, 19, 83, *92*
    Sabha, 16
    Sabratha, 48, 106
    Sirte, 64, *64*, 71, *71*
    Tarhuna, 19, 83
    Tobruk, 24, 69, 70, 76
civil war, *10*, 63–64, *64*, 65, 124
climate, 16, 23, 25, 26–27, *26*, *27*,
    29, 41
clothing, 120–121, *120*, *121*, *122*
coastline, 15, 16, 17, *17*, *18*, 24, 85,
    113
constitution, 55
construction industry, 79
Copper Souk, *100*
Coptic Orthodox Church, *92*
couscous (national dish), 116–117,
    116
crafts, *100*, 104–105, *104*, *107*
currency (dinar), 76, *76*
Cyrenaica region
    Akhdar Mountains, 24–25, *24*
    Arab arrival in, 50
    Benghazi in, 24
    climate of, 27
    coastline in, 24
    Derna in, 24
    Greeks in, 46
    Muhammad Idris al-Sanusi in, 56
    mujahideen in, 54
    oil discovery in, 57

Sanusi Brotherhood in, 52
    Tobruk in, 24
Cyrene colony, 48

D
date palm trees, *14*, 19, 40–41, *40*, 72
Derna, 24
dinar (currency), 76, *76*

E
economy
    agriculture and, 77, 78–79
    civil war and, 65, *74*
    construction industry, 79
    corruption in, 76
    currency (dinar), 76, *76*
    employment, 58, 75, 76–77, 84,
        86, 115, 122
    exports, 57, *57*
    government and, 69, 76
    manufacturing, 77, 79
    mining, 77
    oil industry, 19, 57–58, *57*, 61, 65,
        70, *74*, 75, 76–77
    sanctions, 60, 61
    taxes, 50
    tourism, 19
    trade, 9, *44*, 45, 46, 60, 61, 81, 91
    tributes, 51
    Tripoli and, 72
education, 58, 69, *104*, 115, 123,
    124–126, *124*, *125*, 127
Education Ministry, 127
Eid al-Adha (Feast of the Sacrifice),
    94
Eid al-Fitr (End of Ramadan), 94
elections, 66, 67
electricity, 31, 65, 75, 115
elevation, 16, 21, 22
El-Kaleh, Rami, 109
employment, 58, 75, 76–77, 84, 86,
    115, 122

estivation, 35
European colonization, 52–55, *55*
exports, 57, *57*
Exxon company, 57

F
families, *114*, 115, 121–123
fashion, 105, 121, *121*
fast foods, 119, *119*
al-Fateh University. *See* University of
    Tripoli.
fennec fox, *32*, 37
Fezzan region
    Arab people in, 50
    Garamantes Empire in, 47, 48,
        49, *49*
    geography of, 22
    oases, 22, 24
    sand dunes, 22
    Tibesti Mountains, 22
film industry, 102
Five Pillars of Islam, 95–96
flooding, 27, *29*
foods, 35, 40, *40*, 86, 97, 98, 116–117,
    117, 118, *118*, 119, *119*
foosball (game), *126*
foreign workers, 84–85, *84*, *85*
fossils, 23
France, 53, 64
fruits, 117, *117*

G
Gabriel (angel), 90
games, 126, *126*
Garamantes Empire, *45*, 47, 48, 49, *49*
General National Congress (GNC),
    69
geography
    borders, 15, 22
    caves, 16
    coastline, 15, 16, 17, *17*, *18*
    deserts, 15, 21, 22, *22*, 23, 25

jewelry, *107*
Judaism, 92

K

Karamanli Mosque, *105*
kasrah (flatbread), 117
Khalifa, Asma, 12–13
Kufra Oasis, 25

L

languages, 50, 86, *86*, 87, *87*, 93
Leptis Magna, 46, *47*, 48, 106
Libyan Desert, *22*, 25, *34*, 38, 39, 57, 59
Libyan Military College, 59
Libyan Premier League, 112
literature, 101, 102, 103–104, *103*
livestock, 25, 43, 78, 117
Lockerbie bombing, 60, *60*
lunar calendar, 93, 94
Luxembourg Peace Prize, 12–13

M

Mandara Lakes, *14*
manufacturing, 77, 79
maps. *See also* historical maps.
    Berber-language areas, *86*
    geopolitical, *11*
    population density, *82*
    resources, *79*
    topographical, *16*
    Tripoli, *72*
Marcus Aurelius, emperor of Rome, 46–47
marriage, 121–122, *122*
Martyrs' Square, *72*, 96
Mattawa, Khaled, 103, 104
Mawlid al-Nabawi (Muhammad's birthday), 99
Mecca, Saudi Arabia, 89, 90–91, 93, 96, *96*, 97, *97*
Medina, Saudi Arabia, 91, 93

Mediterranean Sea, 15, *17*, 53, 81, 85, 86
metalwork, *100*, 104
metric system, 79
migrants, 83, 84–86, *84*, *85*
military, 47, 58, 59, 70, 73
mining, 77
Misrata, 19, 83, 92
mosques, 90, 95, *100*, *105*
Muhammad (prophet), 89–90, *90–91*, 93, 97–98, *99*, 110
Muharram (first month), 93
mujahideen ("freedom fighters"), 54
al-Mukhtar, Omar, 54, *54*, 76, 94, 109, 133, *133*
Murabit, Alaa, 99, *99*, 133
music, 101, 107–111, *108*, *109*, 133
Muslims. *See* Islamic religion.

N

Nafusa Mountains, 20–21, *21*
Nasser, Gamal Abdel, 59
national animal, 37
national anthem, 68
national dish, 116–117, *116*
national flag, 73, *73*
national flower, 41, *41*
national holidays, 120
National Museum, 72, 106, *106*, 127
National Transitional Council, 64
natural gas, 77
negayza (game), 126
nocturnal animals, 35
nomadic people, 59, 82–83, 108
Norman people, 50
North Atlantic Treaty Organization (NATO), 30–31
Norwegian Students' and Academics' International Assistance Fund, 12

O

oases, *14*, 22, 24, 40–41

oil industry, 19, 57–58, *57*, 61, 65, 70, *74*, 75, 76–77
olives, 19, 20, 78
Operation Dignity, 70
Ottoman Empire, 50, 52
oud (musical instrument), 108, *108*

P

palm trees, *14*, 19, 40–41, *40*, 72
para-phenylenediamine, 123
people
    Almohads, 50
    ancestors, 82
    Arabs, 49–50, *50*, 82
    arranged marriages, 121–122
    Barbary pirates, 51, *51*
    Bedouin, 83
    Berbers, 44, 45, 50, 82
    Carthaginians, 45–46, *45*, 91
    children, *18*, 30, 65, *94*, *114*, 123, 124–126, *126*, *127*
    clothing, 120–121, *120*, *121*, 122
    diversity of, 81
    education, 58, 69, *104*, 115, 123, 124–126, *124*, *125*, 127
    employment, 58, 75, 76–77, 84, 86, 115, 122
    families, *114*, 115, 121–123
    foods, 35, 40, *40*, 86, 97, 98, 116–117, *117*, 118, *118*, 119, *119*
    foreign workers, 84–85, *84*, *85*
    games, 126, *126*
    Garamantes, *45*, 47, 48, 49, *49*
    Greeks, 46, 48, 106
    health care, 86, 115
    housing, 58, *106*, 122, 123
    immigration, 83, 84–86, *84*, *85*
    languages, 50, 86, *86*, 87, *87*, 93
    marriage, 121–122, *122*
    migrants, 83, 84–86, *84*, *85*
    nomads, 59, 82–83, 108
    Normans, 50

water
  animal life and, 37
  Great Man-Made River, 29–31,
    30, 78
  irrigation, 25, *25*, 28–29, 78
  seawater, 28, *28*, 29
  wadis (riverbeds), 20, 28
  wells, 28–29
water sports, 113
weights and measures, 79
wells, 28–29
"We Will Not Surrender" (Rami El-
  Kaleh), 109
wildflowers, 24–25, *24*, 41
women
  clothing, 105, 120–121, *121*
  employment of, 123
  henna tattoos, 123, *123*
  Islamic religion and, 99, 120–121
  marriage, 121–123, *122*
  Voice of Libyan Women (VLW),
    99
  Tripoli, *31*, 80
  voting rights, 66
World Heritage Sites, 48, *48*, 106
World War I, 54
World War II, 19, 55

z
zakat (charitable works), 97
zawiyas (lodges), 52
Zayd ibn Thabit (scribe), 110–111

Meet the Author

TERRI WILLIS HAS A DEGREE IN JOURNALISM FROM the University of Wisconsin–Madison. She is the author of many books for young people, mostly dealing with geography and environmental issues. She has written several titles in the Enchantment of the World series, including *Lebanon*, *Afghanistan*, *Kuwait*, *Qatar*, *Venezuela*, *Romania*, *Vietnam*, and *Democratic Republic of the Congo*. Willis lives in Cedarburg, Wisconsin.

Willis was excited to begin research for this book. "This is the third time I've written a book on Libya, so I'm quite familiar with the way the country ran under Muammar Qaddafi. But to really dig into how things are today after Qaddafi's death has been fascinating," she says. "He was such a dominant force in the country. Qaddafi influenced so many aspects of life during his reign. From the economy to foreign relations to music in the streets, he was in charge."

"Now, even though he's been dead for years, the hole his absence left is having an equally thorough grasp on the country. It's sad to see how the optimism felt by so many right after his death has turned into frustration, hardship, and sorrow. Life remains so difficult for the people of Libya. But there's still hope for the future. I'm encouraged to see that young people are leading the way, with a promise of more peaceful times ahead."

Photo Credits

Photographs ©:

cover: Bashar Shglila/Getty Images; back cover: Paul Doyle/Alamy Images; 2: Avalon/Photoshot License/ Alamy Images; 5: Eric Lafforgue/age fotostock; 6 right: Paul Doyle/Alamy Images; 6 left: imageBROKER/ Alamy Images; 6 center: Angela Prati/age fotostock; 7 left: Charles O. Cecil/Alamy Images; 7 right: Jorge Tutor/Alamy Images; 8: blickwinkel/Alamy Images; 10: Mohammed el-Shaiky/AP Images; 12: REUTERS/ Alamy Images; 13: Charles O. Cecil/Alamy Images; 14: Kreder Katja/age fotostock; 17: Gary Cook/Alamy Images; 18: Charles O. Cecil/Alamy Images; 19 bottom: Constantinos Pliakos/Alamy Images; 19 top: Wolfgang Kaehler/Superstock, Inc.; 20: Charles O. Cecil/Alamy Images; 21: Jorge Tutor/Alamy Images; 22: Konrad Wothe/Minden Pictures; 23: Roberto Esposti/Alamy Images; 24: Charles O. Cecil/Alamy Images; 25: Claudius Thiriet/Biosphoto/Minden Pictures; 26: REUTERS/Alamy Images; 27: LOOK Die Bildagentur der Fotografen GmbH/Alamy Images; 28: imageBROKER/Alamy Images; 29: MAHMUD TURKIA/ AFP/Getty Images; 30: Barry Iverson/Alamy Images; 31: Abdel Magid Al Fergany/AP Images; 32: Konrad Wothe/Minden Pictures; 34: Herbert Hopfensperger/age fotostock; 35: Paul Doyle/Alamy Images; 36: Jochen Tack/Getty Images; 37: Rebecca Jackrel/Alamy Images; 38: Herbert Hopfensperger/age fotostock; 39: DAVID J SLATER/Alamy Images; 40: frans lemmens/Alamy Images; 41: Alonso Aguilar/Alamy Images; 42: José Fuste Raga/age fotostock; 44: DeAgostini/Getty Images; 47: SuperStock/age fotostock; 48 bottom: Robert Preston Photography/Alamy Images; 48 top: Paul Doyle/Alamy Images; 49: LOOK Die Bildagentur der Fotografen GmbH/Alamy Images; 51: Niday Picture Library/Alamy Images; 52: Classic Vision/age fotostock; 53: SZ Photo/Scherl/The Image Works; 54: Pictures From History/The Image Works; 55: AP Images; 56: AP Images; 57: Pictorial Parade/Archive Photos/Getty Images; 58: Roger-Viollet/The Image Works; 59: ZUMA Press, Inc./Alamy Images; 60: ROY LETKEY/AFP/Getty Images; 62: Barry Iverson/ Alamy Images; 63: REUTERS/Alamy Images; 64: epa european pressphoto agency b.v./Alamy Images; 65: Mohammad Hannon/AP Images; 66: Abdel Magid Al Fergany/AP Images; 68: REUTERS/Alamy Images; 69: MAHMUD TURKIA/AFP/Getty Images; 70: epa european pressphoto agency b.v./Alamy Images; 71: Xinhua/Alamy Images; 72 top: JTB MEDIA CREATION, Inc./Alamy Images; 73: Gil C/Shutterstock; 74: REUTERS/Alamy Images; 76: Ivan Vdovin/Alamy Images; 78: REUTERS/Alamy Images; 80: Paul Doyle/ Alamy Images; 83: DEA/M G MARCHELLI/age fotostock; 84: Melbo/age fotostock; 85: ARIS MESSINIS/ AFP/Getty Images; 87: Paul Doyle/Alamy Images; 88: Eric Lafforgue/age fotostock; 90: Charles O. Cecil/ Alamy Images; 91: Sophiejames/Dreamstime; 92: REUTERS/Alamy Images; 93: V_ctoria/Shutterstock; 94: REUTERS/Alamy Images; 95: REUTERS/Alamy Images; 96: epa european pressphoto agency b.v./Alamy Images; 97: HASSAN AMMAR/AFP/Getty Images; 98: REUTERS/Alamy Images; 99: GIANLUIGI GUERCIA/AFP/Getty Images; 100: Robert J Preston/Alamy Images; 102: REUTERS/Alamy Images; 103: REUTERS/Alamy Images; 104: Paul Doyle/Alamy Images; 105: Charles O. Cecil/Alamy Images; 106 top: Angela Prati/age fotostock; 106 bottom: Marka/Superstock, Inc.; 107: Nico Tondini/age fotostock; 108: gulfimages/Superstock, Inc.; 109: NASSER YOUNES/AFP/Getty Images; 110: REUTERS/Alamy Images; 111: REUTERS/Alamy Images; 112: REUTERS/Alamy Images; 113: REUTERS/Alamy Images; 114: imageBROKER/Alamy Images; 116: MAHMUD TURKIA/AFP/Getty Images; 117: REUTERS/Alamy Images; 118: Simon Reddy/Alamy Images; 119: dpa picture alliance/Alamy Images; 120: Angela Prati/age fotostock; 121: Brian Ach/Getty Images; 122: ZUMA Press, Inc./Alamy Images; 123: Boaz Rottem/Alamy Images; 124: Charles O. Cecil/Alamy Images; 125: Patti McConville/Alamy Images; 126 top: REUTERS/ Alamy Images; 126 bottom: Nasser Nasser/AP Images; 127: Egmont Strigl/imageBROKER/age fotostock; 130 left: Constantinos Pliakos/Alamy Images; 131 top: Gil C/Shutterstock; 131 bottom: Jorge Tutor/Alamy Images; 132 bottom: Ivan Vdovin/Alamy Images; 132 top: SuperStock/age fotostock; 133 bottom: Pictures From History/The Image Works; 133 top: Charles O. Cecil/Alamy Images.

Maps by Mapping Specialists.